PRAISE FOR
Beyond the PIG and the APE

"Krishna takes esoteric wisdom and makes it practical, merging the so-called Eastern mystical outlook — or as he calls it, 'in-look' — with the scientific logic of the West. In my own life, formerly as a business CEO and now as a teacher of management, I have found that inner personal growth and effective decision-making go hand in hand: Krishna's book is a guide to both."

— John Rehfeld
Author, *Alchemy of a Leader*
Executive MBA Faculty, Pepperdine and University of San Diego

"This wonderful book provides a simple, clear and wise road map to overcoming our blocks to happiness and fulfillment. A thoroughly pleasurable read; it's a user-friendly guide to help the reader achieve a state of lasting joy and contentment in the midst of life's challenges. Enjoy!"

— Olivia Mellan
Psychotherapist and money coach
Author, *Money Harmony*

"As an Indian raised on a diet of spiritual ideas and a technology entrepreneur raised on a diet of dozens of business and self-improvement books, I thought I knew what I was doing. What I didn't realize until I read Krishna's book was how ineffective my vocabulary was for understanding the workings of my own mind. Krishna's metaphors are simple and yet vivid and hence incredibly powerful. They have created a language I now use to be aware of how I make choices and decisions in all aspects of my life, every day. I've become aware of my APE, PIG and Ego, and I have caught them red-handed, wreaking havoc with my decision making! A must have for everyone."

— **Venkat Krishnamurthy**
Serial Entrepreneur, Academy Award winner, Family man

"Beyond the PIG and the APE is a highly readable, profound and practical guide toward mental health and well being. I believe deeply that people are meant to be happy, so why are so many miserable? This book actually shows how to transcend the misery and get to happiness. A person living the kind of happiness Krishna describes is someone comfortable in his or her own skin, a person that others want to be around."

— **Sharon Eakes**
Executive Coach
Co-author, *Liberating Greatness*
Former vice president, Gateway Rehab®

"The framework presented in this book works great for making both complex and simple decisions in business and in personal life. Krishna's concepts of the PIG and the APE are not only fun to read about, they are true to life and easy to apply."

— **Ashok Trivedi**
Co-founder and Co-Chairman
iGATE Corporation

BEYOND THE PIG AND THE APE

"The path to be pursued is poorly lit by a flickering consciousness"
— Albert Einstein

BEYOND THE
PIG
AND THE
APE

Realizing
SUCCESS
and true
HAPPINESS

KRISHNA PENDYALA
with **Mike Vargo**

Foreword by Marc Allen

Big YOU Media
Allison Park, PA

ISBN: 0615435297
ISBN-13: 9780615435299
Library of Congress Control Number: 2011903859

Illustrations by Justin Cooper.
Author's photo by Matt Polk.

To Hal
The happiest man I know

And to my family
Sangeetha, Nyan and Lehka
Thank you for teaching me something every day.

CONTENTS

5: BECOMING AWARE

Life is a maze of obstacles and illusions until we become highly aware. This pivotal chapter describes the stages of awareness that can lead us to insight and joy.

6: WHAT'S DRIVING YOU?

We've seen how our inner creatures can get in our way, and seen that awareness is the way through. With this chapter we begin applying the concepts for practical results.

7: MAKING CHOICES

Every so often, we have to make big decisions. And every day, we make myriad "little" choices that add up to shape the fabric of our lives. The principles in this chapter apply to both kinds.

8: EXPANDING CREATIVITY

*Creativity is neither a dark art nor a simple set of mind-tricks.
However, each of us can learn to be more creative, more often
— both in our work and in daily life.*

9: THE STATE OF JOY

*Imagine living in harmony with life, not constantly feeling frustrated by it
or worrying about it. As we become less driven by our animal instincts and
our Egos, we grow ever more open to this great gift: the state of profound joy.*

A collection of 21 stories, showing how our levels of awareness
affect us in the "Life Spaces" we inhabit.

FOREWORD

These truths seem all too self-evident: Most of us are under a lot of stress. We often feel that our work is too demanding and our personal lives are chaotic. We think we would really like a much more relaxed and enjoyable life — but it's all so hard, with the many difficulties we face in our busy modern world.

Then someone like Krishna Pendyala comes along to challenge these views. He dares to speak of creating lasting happiness, right here, right now. A busy and successful person himself, he says it is possible to find profound joy and inner peace, not by "escaping" from our lives but by living at a higher level of awareness. If you don't think it can happen in your life, you might change your mind when you read this book.

Lasting fulfillment is not only possible, Krishna Pendyala tells us, it is our birthright. And the steps to reaching this wonderful state of happiness, inner peace and contentment are not all that difficult. One of Krishna's strengths is showing us how simple it can be. His clear little diagrams alone are worth the price of admission. When I first saw those illustrations, I told him he had put the great concepts of Eckhart Tolle's The Power of Now into a simple form. Eckhart Tolle is my favorite writer of all time, so these are words of praise.

Every generation needs new writers and speakers to remind us of the age-old truths that lead to a better life experience. With this book, Krishna Pendyala emerges as a voice of clarity and sanity in a crazy, stress-filled world. As he likes to say, "We have been conditioned to focus on misguided goals — success at any cost in business and instant happiness in personal life." To learn a path that is far more fruitful, read on. Krishna has written the best kind of book: one that can improve your life and your world in a great many remarkable ways.

— **Marc Allen**
Co-founder, New World Library
Author, Visionary Business
Publisher, The Power of Now

Chapter 1
ARE YOU HAPPY?

If you like films, as I do, you might have seen a romantic comedy that was a hit some years ago, a French movie called *Cousin, Cousine.* There's an unforgettable little scene that leaps out from amid the farce and the froth.

Girl and guy are deliriously in love. It's a beautiful day and they're off on a motorcycle ride, guy in the front and girl hanging on from behind. They've got the wind in their hair and they're laughing as they fly along a country road, when up ahead they see a farmer working in his field. They pull over. The girl leans towards the farmer.

It seems she has a question for him: "Are you happy?"

Now the camera goes tight on the farmer. He's a man well into middle age. For a moment, he considers this question that has come out of the blue. You can almost see the memories of a lifetime rippling across his sun-crinkled face while he considers.

And there's no mistaking the expression on his face as he reaches the verdict. No need to answer in words. The bitter scowl and the weary shaking of the head say it all: *Happy? You've got to be kidding. I'm so out of touch with "happy" that I hardly know what it means any more.*

When the movie is shown in a theater, a curious thing happens at this point. The audience explodes with laughter. The scene is a laugh because for many of us, that answer hits oh, so close to home. And in the fantasy space of a movie theater, it is *possible* to laugh when it's somebody up on the screen, not you, who has to admit the sad, sad fact.

But then after the movie ends, then what? When it's time to go back to life? What will you do now?

That was the question I faced as a young man, some thirty years ago. Not coming out of a movie theater, but in a hospital bed in India, coming out of a coma after my third suicide attempt.

The Turning Point

People couldn't understand why I was unhappy. As the cliché says, I had so much going for me. I was a college student at IIT, the famed Indian Institute of Technology, having been the one kid in a hundred who scores high enough on the entrance exam to get in. On graduating I would join the most envied class of people in India, the few able to earn a good living or get an entry visa to America. Supposedly the game plan was clear. All I had to do was stick to my work, like that French farmer. Then I would succeed at school and succeed in my career, and success, of course, would make me happy.

The notion that life might actually work the other way around — that if you first learn to be happy, you are more likely to succeed at whatever you do — had not occurred to me or to anyone urging me on. This illumination didn't come until much later. Meanwhile I seemed to be mired in a state far worse than the usual teenager's moodiness.

I was suffering inside my skin and suffering above all in my head. I couldn't understand it myself. "Wounded idealism" seemed to have something to do with it, because the most trivial upsets would devastate me. For instance, I was a generous soul, always doing things like letting other students borrow my bicycle. Once, a friend in my dorm got angry because I wouldn't lend him the bike at a time when I needed it myself. Instead of thinking what most of us would — *well, now we know what a jerk this person can be* — I turned the incident into yet another tragic confirmation of the horrible state of the universe. Over which, I tormented myself endlessly.

There's no justice. I think people are nice, and I try to be nice to them, but they're selfish and wicked ... How can I trust anyone? And me, what's wrong with me? I play by the rules and I don't get the payback. What are the rules in this stupid life anyway?

That's just a small sound bite from a long-playing inner monologue. I was constantly agonizing over all sorts of things. From time to time I'd escape into drinking and drugs, but that only fed a downward spiral that left me behind in my work and in a deeper depression. If you have been caught up in a routine of this type you know it's no way to live. It's exhausting.

For my third attempt I tried the long train ride to nowhere. That's the method where you load up with pills, buy a one-way ticket on a long-distance train with sleeper berths, and climb into a bed with no intention of awakening. It seemed like the perfect exit strategy. What it became was the turning point.

I did awaken.

And since then, I have learned some things about happiness, which I'd like to share with you in this book. Before we go on, however, I have three requests.

Three Favors You Can Do for Yourself

First, please don't expect a secret of happiness that will arrive in a flash of enlightenment, instantly changing your life. I'm not a guru who can promise such a product. It took me many years after that wake-up day — years of gradual learning, with continued struggles — to get to the point where I now am, which includes coaching others and being comfortable enough in my own perspective on happiness to write about the subject.

But your journey doesn't have to take quite as long. If you'd rather save a few decades, you may gain some insights from this book that can help.

Second, if you are seriously or chronically unhappy, stuck in patterns of life that keep repeating like a bad top-40 song played over and over, please don't assume that just reading books will be enough to get you out of the rut. At crucial times in my life I've had the guidance of caring and experienced people: a wise grandfather, an equally wise advisor, an expert professional counselor. There's no substitute for human help *as long as you get it from humans who can actually help.* Often, this means help from a professional. Another rule of thumb I've heard is to turn to people "who have what you want" — people who show the kind of happiness, the freedom from craving and torment, that you would like.

What's available in this book is a way of looking at things — specifically, a way of looking within — which may be useful. And it's meant to be useful no matter where you are on the road to happiness and success: starting out, somewhere in the middle, or in the stage called "doing pretty well, but it still seems that something is off." Wherever you are, I applaud you for taking the initiative to go further.

Finally, please don't attempt what I attempted, by the long train ride or by any method. It would be wonderful to meet you one of these days to hear whether the book had value for you, and that will work best if both of us are alive.

Now back to the wake-up call.

Stages on the Road to Happiness

Maybe you've read some of the tough-guy detective novels where the hero describes coming to, after he's been drugged or beaten. "A hundred jackhammers were tap-dancing inside my skull. My body felt trampled by angry elephants," and so on. Having come out of that coma, all I can tell you is: no exaggeration.

It turned out I'd been drugged *and* beaten. I had drugged myself, and also bore evidence of use as a target for martial arts practice. It's possible that before I was found and rushed to the hospital by a railroad employee to whom I am ever grateful, somebody had tried to slug and kick me out of my stupor, and got carried away. Such things are known to happen in India.

At any rate I did not awake to the bluebird of happiness chirping at the window. My first thought was, *I can't even kill myself.* But after that I received a rare gift, although it often seemed like a miserable ordeal. Recuperation was slow. I had a paralyzed left leg and other injuries. While they healed, I spent six months in bed. This gave me plenty of time to reflect — more time for introspection, at the age of 18, than some people take in all their years. Eventually I reached a conclusion: *It looks like I am destined to live in this world, so I had better learn how.*

That was the real turning point, simply resolving to learn how to live. The motive at the time was mainly selfish. Only later did it dawn on me that there are broader benefits, that when you're happy you are better able to make others happy. And let's now boil down the rest of my own story to a few items you may find relevant.

At first I figured I was unhappy because others were running my life. Like many young people — and many not so young — I'd been trying to live up to my parents' expectations and succeed by societal standards. So I decided I had to play society's games but set my own goals, and succeed on my own terms.

That was in 1981 and that game plan went better. I did finish my IIT degree and move to the U.S., where I am now a citizen, but I switched fields, from engineering into film and video. During the 1990s, I started two visual-media companies, marrying technology with my love of those media. Although neither startup made me rich and famous, most people would say I did rather well. Better yet I married a wonderful woman, with whom I now have two amazing children.

Yet all through these years my internal state was very much a work in progress. And I literally worked on it, often as hard as on outward success: reading over 400 books on personal growth, going to therapy, taking self-improvement classes and seminars. "The pursuit of happiness" indeed! During that chase I moved through several stages, some of which you may find familiar.

> *Youthful idealism* was where I had started, long ago in India. Back then I had a simplistic world view based on assumptions like these: Life is fair and people are nice. If I just follow the course laid out for me, I may have to work hard, but life will be "easy" in the sense that all due rewards will come. I'll be a successful dude and a happy and benevolent saint as well. Hah!

The wake-up call then swung the pendulum the other way.

> Goodbye innocent idealism, so easily wounded, and hello to *blatant self-preservation*. Basic assumptions here: People are twisted and so is the world. You've got to play the game for what it's worth, have your own agenda and go after it.

7

This is a grasping and dodging stage — grab what you can, dodge those bullets. Some people stay in it for a lifetime. It can keep you fired up but also burn you out — high energy, wrong fuel. It's pain covered by agitation, and the suffering continues. Upon coming to the U.S., I met plenty of fellow sufferers caught in the same stage. But my misery didn't love that company, so ...

> ➤ *Resignation to the trials of life* came next. I remember coming across Scott Peck's book *The Road Less Traveled.* The very first sentence — "Life is difficult" — was somehow a comforting revelation. *Aha, he says life is inherently hard. Then I haven't been missing the "easy" answers; there aren't any. I guess I can live with that.* Also, I began going to a therapist, who told me, "You see everything black and white. I'd like to help you see the shades in between." In other words, life is neither ideal nor rotten; it just sort of is what it is.

All of this helped to ease the pain but brought little positive joy. For me, the net result of the painkilling was "Life is blah." So, onward and upward. I became a *student of happiness,* joining the many for whom it's an ongoing course of study.

> ➤ *The systematic pursuit of the positive* was a stage that lasted a long time. I devoured what I now call "method" books: methods for happy living, with seven steps to such-and-such or forty-two ways to improve your whatever. I turned into a positive-thinking fiend. In this stage, you work hard

at using your thinking to manage your thinking, and to manage your feelings — managing them into a better state.

Much of that helped, too. A lot of it was necessary. But it still left me in the state of not-quite-there, something's off. Life remained an enigma. It remained ... well, difficult, albeit less so.

Then came the final stage, in which I was drawn to a more transcendental or mystical approach. This approach is typified in the kinds of books that say: Life doesn't have to be such a chore. Happiness isn't something you have to chase. *You just have to look within.*

Which is excellent advice. But unfortunately, most of what I was reading and hearing at this stage tended to be pretty abstract. It left one little practical question hanging.

In Search of What to Look For

Once you've learned that you need to look within to find real happiness, what exactly do you look for?

It's not as if somewhere down in the vault there is a safe-deposit box marked "happiness." In fact, there's an awful lot within. A person could go digging around indefinitely, aided by teams of psycho-archaeologists. Or spend years in the lotus position without finding the magic lotus blossom. Perhaps a simple guide to looking would be nice? Maybe not to spell it all out, but, you know, to help focus the search?

This book reflects what finally brought the picture together for me, put into the simplest terms possible. It's based on what has worked for me, and for many of the fine people I now deal with in my present capacities as a personal coach and leader of seminars on change and inner awareness. I believe that the concepts and principles I am presenting have a firm basis in science, too. At various places in the book, to help illustrate a point or support what I'm saying, you will see references to scientific findings from biology, psychology, and other fields.

But this is not a book of scientific theories. It's a book about real life, as lived by people like you and me. Above all I have tried to make it clear and practical.

The next chapter gives a view of the goal — real, profound happiness — so we can have a clearer idea of what we're looking for. Then we'll move on to how to look, listen, and experience our way to the goal.

And one more thing, very important. This isn't only about what to look for. It's also about what to look out for.

Chapter 2
LASTING HAPPINESS

What is "happiness" anyway? Rather than weigh us down with a textbook definition, I'll simply try to describe what deep, profound, and lasting happiness looks like, and feels like.

A Picture of Happiness

For openers we can put aside a stereotype. The common picture of a profoundly happy, enlightened soul is someone who is "liberated" from all the demands and desires of this world, renouncing the rat race to go off to the mountains and meditate in bliss. Only a few of us can live this way. Nor is it necessary. Profound happiness is within reach, right in the middle of so-called everyday life, and it looks something like this:

You have wants and hopes that you're working towards, but it's not a rat race. In this state of happiness you don't worry about every little outcome or get tied in knots over difficulties. When things don't go as planned, you just accept what life presents you and take it from there.

A happy person has plenty of energy, and it's healthy energy. Very little of it gets burned up in the form of tension, craving, regret, fear, anger, or inner turmoil of any kind. You're not run by those nagging inner voices that can chatter in our heads and churn our insides. Instead, you operate from a sense of calm and clarity.

Of course you'll still make mistakes. But often you will find yourself making choices that seem inspired — and rarely will you sabotage yourself by doing the stupid, impulsive things that can leave us slapping our heads and asking "Why did I do that?"

Of course things will happen in life that you don't want to happen. There are times when even a happy person is sad or dismayed. But you don't sink into a paralyzing funk — certainly not over anything short of a genuine tragedy — and you sense that even the darkest times would be emotionally survivable.

Those are some highlights. Now let's pick out a few underlying traits. For instance, this kind of happiness is not *conditional*. It doesn't depend on circumstances. You are happy because you belong to life, not because of what belongs to you.

It's a "realistic" state of being, not some positive-thinking dreamland, but one grounded in an awareness of what is, right now.

You might also call it a "unified" state. A happy person isn't torn by civil wars going on inside.

And perhaps you have spotted a certain pattern in what's written above. For a guy describing happiness, I've used a lot of negatives. *It's not this, it's the absence of that,* et cetera.

A reader may ask, "But what about all the good stuff? What do I *get*?"

Well, that's up to you. Or you might say it comes to you, once the interference is out of the way. Instead of hearing noise and static, and feeling the pressure, you're able hear the birds in the morning ... smell the roses without forcing yourself to "stop" to smell them ... and see, taste and feel the beauty all around you.

You might even hear the little birdie that's been trying to tell you something. In other words, in this state of happiness we are able to make truly creative choices. We are no longer subject to the creatures that live within each of us, making choices that can undermine our happiness.

Occupied by Aliens?

Wait a minute! What's this about creatures within us?

That's right. I discovered them and you will, too. They were the ones holding me back during the long years when I thought that I was doing things "my way," and yet wondered why I still wasn't happy.

I discovered that my inner planet — the sphere of existence that I liked to call "me" — was under occupation. There were creatures in there living my life for me, making choices for me, without my knowing it.

This discovery, creepy as it may sound, opened a door that I now invite you to step through. We'll be going on a journey within, and the mission is simple. One word sums it up.

Awareness

Just by becoming aware of our inner creatures, we can begin to see how they make choices for us that defeat our chances for lasting happiness. These choices range from little follies like numbing our senses in front of the TV, to ill-conceived major decisions about our work, the people in our lives, and *who we are.*

Being aware of what the creatures are up to can then open us to a larger level of awareness — the level at which we know who we really are and are fully present.

And that's about all there is to it. The journey includes very little in the way of tricks or techniques for dealing with these creatures, and only some very simple and basic ideas about making better choices.

In short, you won't come away with a set of recipes for living happily. Instead, you will find that recipes are not what you need. Once you become aware, you'll be capable of creating — or finding — your own state of happiness. Which is what we all have to do ultimately.

The journey to that lift-off stage is called *An Inner-Space Odyssey.* Its purpose is to have you reach a level of awareness at which you can have profound happiness in your own way, without as many mis-steps or the depth of suffering that I had to go through.

The only trick, if you can call it that, is using the right animal stories ...

Chapter 3
THE ANIMALS WITHIN

Every culture uses animal stories to teach lessons about life. There is one story so old that no one knows how old it is, and it is told nearly everywhere. Here in America it's called The Grasshopper and the Ant, but in India, where I learned it as a child, we knew it as The Cricket and the Ant.

Cricket was a happy fellow — or so it seemed. All day long he did whatever he pleased, singing his songs, dancing and feasting upon the delicacies of the field. Meanwhile his neighbor Ant was busy working. All day long she trudged back and forth from the fields to her nest, carrying grains and leaves that were bigger than herself — how does she do that? — and stashing them away for the future. Cricket urged her to stop and play. You're missing the best part of life, he said. You should worry less about tomorrow and enjoy today!

Ant would have none of it. She didn't even reply. She just kept marching her rounds, as methodically as her six legs could carry her, until Cricket shrugged and went back to his games.

Then came the cold season. And while Ant was snug and well fed, Cricket began to struggle. Each day there was less and less food to be had. The cold air slowed his energetic singing to a whimper. On the day when his song was no longer heard, all the animals knew that Cricket, alas, was no more.

The message of the story is a good one: we should think ahead and work for the future, not just seek pleasure in the moment. However it's a story that leaves a lot of people feeling uneasy. It becomes part of our conditioning in early childhood, and then as we grow older we begin to wonder:

Ant is supposed to be the hero but who wants to be like Ant? She comes across as a total drudge. Her life is *boring*. As for Cricket, who chose the fun-filled lifestyle, he's *dead*. Children and adults alike may well ask: are these the only choices? To be a terminal bubblehead or a grim and joyless Scrooge, damned if we do or don't? *What kind of universe is this, with no good options?*

For a long time in my life I acted as if these options were in fact the only two. I tried being a good little Ant, working so hard to become an academic whiz that the other kids wondered how I did it, until it nearly drove me nuts. Later I tried escaping into Crickety pleasures, but that wasn't the answer either. And I experimented with various happy mediums which turned out to be not-so-happy mediums.

Eventually I noticed a problem that seems to run through both approaches to life. Either way, you're constantly chasing things and avoiding things. If you're Cricket, you're chasing pleasure while avoiding work and responsibility. If you're Ant, you're chasing success while avoiding your feelings, stuffing them so you won't feel the pain. *Hmm, chasing and avoiding.* That was an interesting clue.

As for trying to strike a happy medium, by sort of "managing" and "balancing" things as rationally as possible: one can get fairly far that way. It was how I embarked on a career path and into a life that many would envy. But constantly trying to manage and balance everything in your life, including yourself, is mentally exhausting. You become a struggler and a juggler.

It behooves us all to look for a higher level. And such a level exists, beyond chasing and avoiding, beyond mind-managed struggling and juggling. At this level it is possible to act with foresight, like the Ant, *and* be filled with profound happiness and joy— not just the Cricket's kind of fair-weather pleasure.

So, bye-bye, Cricket and Ant. This task will require becoming aware of the animals within, who pull the sneaky inside jobs that can throw us off track.

We each have inner drives or instincts that I have labeled the PIG and the APE. Let's see how they operate, starting with our animal relatives after whom they are named.

Meet the PIG

Pigs, both the wild and domestic kinds, are omnivorous scavengers. They will eat almost anything that lies in their path and they will eat as much of it as they can, often throwing their considerable weight around to get what they want. Selective self-restraint isn't a survival instinct they have acquired. In fact, it would be contrary to their nature. For these highly intelligent animals, the grab-it-and-gobble-it strategy is one that works, one that has made them a thriving and successful species.

It shouldn't be surprising that we humans inherited the tendency to grab whatever looks good, quickly, getting as much of it as possible. Our primeval ancestors were also omnivorous scavengers, living in a world where they had to compete with other species for food, territory and security. For early humans, turning loose the inner PIG was a strategy that worked, too.

The PIG has remained a part of our nature to this day. The only trouble is, these are different times, and the PIG is no longer as valuable, or even as appropriate, as it once was. Over the ages we humans have evolved to build societies that run on planning and cooperation. We're thus able to take care of many of our needs much more efficiently than in the old hunt-and-gather days. Yet the greedy PIG in us keeps acting out — often to our detriment, in this new setting.

Have you been to a Black Friday sale? Just as the approach of autumn sends the birds migrating south, the day after Thanksgiving awakens the PIG in millions of Americans and sends them stampeding to the malls. On Black Friday of 2008, at a Walmart on Sunrise Highway in Long Island, the stampede turned lethal. Customers bursting through the doors at the 5 AM opening time trampled a store employee to death.

And though the outcome is not always so tragic, it can be bad, because the PIG is intent on coming home with some goods. Even if the hyped specials are gone — "What, no more HDTVs for $159?" — unruly herds of shoppers who've succumbed to their PIGs will root through the aisles, scrambling for anything that looks like a bargain. So begins an annual orgy of spending that leaves many people with debts they'll be paying for years to come.

Everyone's PIG is different in the details of its behavior. Not all of us have PIGs that get so excited about buying things in stores, for instance. Some people's PIGs are more attracted to rooting through the aisles of life for sex and physical thrills ... or for money, especially easy money! ... or just for glory and recognition. Perhaps there's a PIG in your neighborhood that can't pass up any chance to look important or sound like an expert.

Nearly all PIGs, including mine, will go for a wide variety of things depending on what's available. The common denominator is that each of us has a PIG, and unlike its four-legged namesake, it does not only go after food. It will chase any kind of pleasure, any satisfaction, as long as the reward is close at hand — lying right there in our paths — and can be gotten quickly. PIG is in capital letters because it's an acronym:

PIG = the ever-present drive to **Pursue Instant Gratification.**

Meet the APE

Apes — and here we are talking about the big apes, gorillas — are not the fierce kings of the jungle they're often imagined to be. These massive King Kongs and Queen Kongs have one defining trait: they do not like to be bothered. They sleep half the day and use their tremendous strength to do little more than pick fruits and leaves. They're also shy creatures that live in secluded areas, shying away from contact with other troublesome species, such as humans. But if confronted by anything that looks like a threat, these apes spring into action. They'll instantly turn and flee as fast as their knuckle-walking can carry them, while the alpha male covers the retreat with his own "threat display" — beating his chest, stamping and screaming and pulling any trick he can think of to tell an intruder: *keep away!*

This is another case of smart animals using a strategy that has worked for them. Although many of their habitats are now endangered, the great apes have survived for ages by playing a unique defensive game that reduces the risk in their lives. You might say they have developed their "avoidance mechanisms" to an extreme extent. The apes have grown big enough to discourage most predators and they don't choose to prey on other animals, either, fighting only as a last resort. They avoid all forms of pain, stress and even hard work that might be overly taxing.

Here again, we humans inherited the tendency to avoid stress and pain, and this too is a trait that has long had survival value for us. In the days when life was a physical struggle, it paid to conserve your strength by avoiding exertion when possible. In the days when fearsome predators like saber-toothed tigers roamed the land, it paid to have a quick flight-or-fight response. And the inner APE remains with us to this day.

For instance, we humans, like many creatures, exhibit what is known as the startle response. If we hear a sudden loud noise, we *jump.* Our hearts pound; every nerve and muscle is on edge.

Sudden loud noises often mean danger, so our APEs are wired to instantly mobilize us for flight-or-fight.

You may have felt your APE acting out in other ways, too. Your phone rings. Caller ID says it's that person who has been trying to track you down to ask a big favor. Your APE takes over, lying low until the call passes into voicemail, where it will rest in peace. Or maybe that same person spots you on the sidewalk in town. Predator approaching! But your APE is ready, and before you know it he's made up a quick lie that you find yourself blurting to cover your retreat: "Sorry, late for a meeting! Catch you another time!"

The APE is extremely good at what he does. He covers the bases, covers our tracks and covers them fast ... with practically no conscious effort needed on our part.

APE = the ever-present drive to **Avoid Painful Experiences.**

There are still cases when it really pays to turn loose the APE. But as with the PIG, we have evolved in such a way that the APE inside us is no longer as useful or appropriate as in the past. Let's look at some more examples of how the APE, and the PIG, can put us at a disadvantage in today's world.

Animals Out of Their Element

On a list of most-avoided experiences, going to the dentist or the doctor would have to rank near the top. Many people won't go unless they are in dire pain, because when their APEs and PIGs weigh up the immediate rewards versus the immediate pains and displeasures, they find there's nothing good about it.

You are going to have to sit in the waiting room and wait. It will probably cost you money, even with a decent insurance plan. Once you are seen, the doctor may want to shove needles into your body and the dentist is scarier yet: she might *drill* you. Worst of all, either one of them is liable to give you bad news at the end.

So what's the upshot? Here is Atul Gawande, a noted physician and author, writing about the issue:

> As a surgeon, I've seen some pretty large tumors. I've excised fist-size thyroid cancers from people's necks and abdominal masses bigger than your head. When I do, this is what almost invariably happens: the anesthesiologist puts the patient to sleep, the nurse unsnaps the gown, everyone takes a sharp breath, and someone blurts out, "How could someone let that thing get so huge?"
>
> I try to describe how slowly and imperceptibly it grew. But staring at the beast it has become, no one buys the explanation. Even the patients are mystified. One day they looked in the mirror, they'll say, and the mass seemed to have ballooned overnight. It hadn't, of course. Usually, it's been growing — and, worse, sometimes spreading — for years.
>
> Too often, by the time a patient finally seeks help, I can't help much.

And then Dr. Gawande makes a penetrating observation about humans in general:

> We have no difficulty taking prompt action when faced with a sudden calamity, like a bleeding head wound, say, or a terror-

ist attack. But we are not good at moving against the creeping, more insidious threats — whether a slow-growing tumor, waistline or debt.

What Dr. Gawande is pointing to is a basic shortcoming of the APE, our primary pain-avoider. Being a primitive part of ourselves, the APE has a primitive system for deciding which kinds of threats to attend to. The APE will only try to avoid threats that are *present* and *immediate.* A trip to the doctor's office? Time, money, pain and bad news, all in one visit, right now? That's a no-brainer: forget it!

The APE will *not* try to account for the negative consequences that might lie in the future. Nor will the APE make any sensible comparison such as "hmm, maybe those future negatives could be much worse than what I'm facing now" ... and then decide to face the short-term pain for a chance of long-term gain.

It just isn't in the nature of the APE to do that. And that's what so often gets us into deep waters in the modern world: we are wired for quick fixes but the game has changed.

Research studies have shown people to be hyper-wary of snakes, even harmless ones, but unwilling to do anything about slow-moving and much larger threats like environmental pollution, even if they are convinced that it's a serious danger. As the columnist Nicholas Kristof put it in the *New York Times*, "We're brilliantly programmed to act on the risks that confronted us in the Pleistocene Age. We're less adept with 21st-century challenges."

Pollution, the national debt, personal debt: yes, these may be serious problems. But unless and until they jump right into the

APE's face, the APE won't respond to them. He will sit calmly in the mind's bushes eating a banana while the problems grow. They don't seem nearly as threatening as that guy who walks up to you on the sidewalk to ask a favor, or the boss strolling into your office to ask how your project is going. To dodge *those* pains the APE will quickly display all the energy and cunning at his command.

Adjusting Our Brains from the Primitive State

Which is why, as long as we rely solely on the APE to keep us out of trouble, we're in trouble.

It is also why we can't rely solely on the pleasure-seeking PIG to bring home lasting happiness. In terms of comparing future and present rewards, the PIG is every bit as short-sighted as the APE. In one psychology experiment, the subjects were asked if they would prefer to get $50 right away or $100 in six months. A large majority of these people chose the $50. They passed up a guarantee to get a 100% return in just a few months, if only they were willing to wait.

That's the PIG for you. Being a vestige of our hunt-and-gather days, the PIG wants to gobble the grain, not use it as seed corn. Other experiments with money, including a bunch conducted by real companies selling things in the so-called real world, have shown many of us to be suckers for anything that's offered "free." *Buy this product*, which costs a good bit of money, *and get a free gift*, which isn't worth much. Or buy the super-saver package and get a bundle of extra features *free*. Of course, the cost of the extras has already been factored into the price of the package, and in most cases the package also locks you into using the company's product or service for a long time. But the PIG doesn't care. All it sees is a free lunch, provided it acts now.

And if most people's PIGs are prone to make silly choices like these — blind to the real costs and values of things, even when the figures are spelled out plainly in dollars and cents — how can we expect the PIG to recognize something as intangible as profound and lasting happiness?

Both the PIG and the APE are aspects of what scientists call the "limbic system," a primitive part of our brain that's believed to be very old in evolutionary terms. Commonly this part is referred to as the lizard brain or the reptilian brain, although it is actually a feature of mammals, including us humans. Whatever we call it, it is the seat of basic drives and emotions that can overpower our more sophisticated functions.

We may think we are progressive, modern individuals. Yet to live a full and happy life, much of what we must do consists of adjusting our brains from the primitive state. We must learn to limit the roles we *unconsciously* allow our animal natures to play, which requires becoming *aware* of them.

This is not so easy, as here the plot thickens. Another inner force intervenes.

Chapter 4

THE IMPOSTOR WITHIN

As we've seen, the PIG and the APE both had their origins as survival instincts. Their purpose is to keep us alive by feeding and protecting us. However, we humans operate on a different plane than most animals. Our notion of identity — of who and what we are — is different. We see ourselves as more than physical beings. The "me" that wants to be fed and protected includes more than my body. It includes my Ego.

A Creature That Thinks It's You, But Isn't

Let's take a minute to define what we mean by the Ego. The word "ego" comes straight from Latin, in which it simply means "I" or my "self." But a few centuries ago, this word got borrowed into English and other languages by philosophers, so they could use it to talk about the concept or *idea* of one's self. And that was where an interesting debate arose. Allow me to sum it up for you, in a way that doesn't take too many liberties with history:

> ➤ Said some philosophers: "The meaning of the Ego is perfectly clear. It's *what I think I am.*"

> ➤ Said others: "Wait a minute. You're using two 'I's there, and that's cheating. It's sort of like saying 'a brick is a brick.' We say the Ego is the part of the 'I' that's capable of thinking, of having such ideas, in the first place!"

> ➤ Said still others: "Well, maybe you've both got a point. Maybe the Ego is ... um, um ... *the part of me that thinks it's me?*"

Aha. Very close to home.

Over time, other shades of meaning have crept in. Today some people use "ego" mainly to refer to feelings of pride or self-centeredness, and in Sigmund Freud's system of thought, the word has a special meaning that I won't try to explain. Kindly disregard those other meanings, which have their uses, but not here. Let's stick with what the old-timers said — because if we become fully aware, we can see that there surely does seem to be "a part of me that thinks it's me." I would describe the whole affair as follows.

The Ego is an identity constructed for you by your mind.

Now here's the important point, the one that is hard for many of us to get.

Your Ego isn't you. It's a fictional version, a made-up version.

In fact, our minds make up fictional identities for us all the time. Children's minds do it: *I'm a space captain. I'm a fire dragon.* And you'd better not try to convince them otherwise, when they're in a serious fantasy mode. Adult minds do it too, both knowingly and unknowingly. Our minds make up online identities; they turn some of us into historical re-enactors at Civil War battles or Renaissance fairs. Millions of us have strange identities at Halloween, and if you've ever acted in a play, you took on the identity of a character that the playwright's mind conjured up. Your Ego is a mind-created identity somewhat like these ... but with a couple of major exceptions.

First, your Ego is a "character" that's never offstage. It's always on and it goes with you everywhere, carried by your mind. And second, with those other made-up identities, as long as you are sane you can tell that they aren't you. It is far trickier to tell the difference between the Ego and you. Some of us never notice the difference. We don't notice because the Ego has been created below the level of awareness, by the mind. It's an identity that each of us has made up without ever being aware of doing so.

Your Ego includes *all that it thinks you are,* including many things that really aren't you at all. To give a very simple example: if we have grown up believing that material possessions are important — that the nature and quality of them, in fact, define the person — then we are likely to be more than a little upset when the new car starts picking up a few dents, or when the living-room carpet begins to show stains. We are going to take it personally. Despite the fact that most people will not pay the slightest attention to these imperfections, we are going to think that our reputation and standing in the community have been damaged; literally that *we* have been damaged — because in the mind's eye, our stuff is part of us, or at least says something vital about us. The Ego, the fictional identity that has gotten unknowingly created since childhood, includes "Pamela, Owner of the Perfect Car and Carpet."

Such nonsense can be carried frighteningly far. Heidi Montag, a reality-TV actress, became a poster child for Ego-driven nuttiness in 2009-10 when she had herself utterly remade with cosmetic surgery. Her remake included ten surgeries in one day, probably a record. She had breast implants, a chin and jaw reduction, a "back scoop," nose job, ear job and more. So many surgeries that they bordered on life-threatening; so many that they left her unable to run, move easily, or even be hugged. All done, of course, to correct imperfections that the world hadn't noticed. And here's the most frightening part. She told reporters that these surgeries allowed "the real me" to come out.

The Ego is a *delusion*. In one sense it can be a delusion that feels empowering, because it expands the notion of who we are. If your mind tells you that you are not just a fan of the legendary Super Bowl-winning Pittsburgh Steelers, but a member of "Steeler Nation," hey, that's a cool identity. Practically the same as being a real Steeler! The trouble is, there's always a downside. What if the Steelers lose?

Along with imaginary powers come imaginary vulnerabilities. Your fictional identity can be threatened and hurt, even when *you* aren't. In the end, this made-up identity is a very limiting identity. It constricts us to being what our minds have come to think we are.

The Ego's Minions

And the Ego, which is a potent delusion in its own right, grows even more potent when teamed with the inner animals. The PIG and the APE are the Ego's minions; they are its servants and it is their master. For as far as the PIG and the APE can tell, the fictional impostor *is* you. They may sniff around a little, down in the dark with their primitive senses, and conclude: *there isn't anyone else around who fits the description, is there?*

All of which can put us in quite a pickle. Inside us we have two beasts, the PIG and the APE, striving their utmost at every moment to feed and protect an us who isn't really us. This creates what Eckhart Tolle calls "the blueprint for dysfunction."

Small examples abound. Time and again, for instance, we see people undercut themselves by "apologizing in advance." If you play golf you've seen the guys who show up with *Oh, I haven't played in a month, and my back is sore,* et cetera until you want to club them. I've been at the table when women, including my wife, lay out a deliciously prepared meal with a constant stream of *This is the first time I made this, maybe I overcooked it, there might be too much salt, you don't have to eat it if you don't like it …*

The strategy is called "lowering expectations" but actually it's the APE out in front of the Ego, trying to trample the way clear to remove any chance of the Ego being wounded. All it does is make everybody, including yourself, uneasy, while alerting people to flaws they probably would have ignored.

Or, Pamela's PIG will rush out to buy a new car and a new car-pet — meaning to re-inflate her Ego but instead leading Pamela's friends to mutter: *the girl is crazy. There was nothing wrong with the old ones.*

Friends and family may learn to accept such behaviors, writing them off as minor quirks of a person they still hold dear. Some offenses, though, are not so lightly written off. Our made-up identities include our relationships to other people and what our minds think those relationships "mean," i.e., what they say about us. When the PIG or the APE acts up to serve the Ego in relation-ship territory, the effect is almost always a disaster.

For instance: in each of our lives there's a person close to us who has a habit that causes us embarrassment when we're out in pub-lic. What is it that makes you wish you had a sign saying "I'm not with this person": a boyfriend who tells stupid jokes? A teenager who dresses like a slob? A wife who looks good until she kills the effect by dressing to kill? You've got some equivalent. One day the person does this embarrassing thing at absolutely the wrong time, so you reprimand the culprit in front of everyone. And to your sur-prise, it turns out no one noticed whatever-it-was that embarrassed you, but your nasty remark raises eyebrows all around. Now peo-ple are wondering what *your* problem is. Now there will be hurt feelings and a real problem when you're back in private with the person involved.

In such cases the friend, child or spouse has done something that we think speaks poorly about our choice of a partner or our ability to raise children properly. Our Ego has been threatened and the APE has jumped in, baring its teeth. And the result is pure sabotage. We've now diminished our reputation while throwing a monkey wrench into a close relationship.

It can get worse. You can also be on the receiving end of a PIG-APE-Ego act. Maybe you have a boss at work who's much too quick to take credit for your and other people's brilliant ideas. That's his greedy PIG feeding his Ego, of course. A friend of mine says she has a boss who plays the other end of the game too. This man is the head of a team within the company, and when something goes wrong — as it always does, after he has launched some ill-conceived plan that had no chance of succeeding — he'll put more energy into defending his plan and explaining why it *should* work, if only the team members weren't bungling it, than he put into designing the plan to begin with. That sounds like classic APE: avoiding the up-front effort, but then springing into action to defend the Ego.

Imagine how it feels to work for such a "team leader." Or as my friend says, imagine being married to him. A pattern of this type repeated regularly would make any relationship a nightmare. And things can get much worse. The pattern just described is only one of many possible patterns that can emerge from the PIG and the APE serving the Ego. They are all destructive because they are all *blind animal instincts in the service of pretense.*

... Wait, do I hear an objection from the audience? Someone says that his boss isn't "pretending"? That this manipulator knows precisely what will earn him points so he can move up the ladder, and he's doing it? I wouldn't be so sure. If the people above him have a certain level of awareness, they've seen through his act, though he may not be aware of it himself. They've said: *oh, that's the guy who's always trying shift the blame while he hogs the credit.* And if the people in charge cannot see what's happening? Well, in that case, maybe the whole organization has a larger problem.

Such cases do occur, perhaps all too frequently. Along with cases of whole families, circles of friends, or societies having the same problem: too many PIGs and APEs running blind, in the service of too many Egos trying to pass themselves off as real persons.

Towards the Next Level — and the Next

So what can we do? We can start with ourselves. We can start by looking within, and bringing our own mind-creatures — the PIG, the APE, the Ego — into the *light of awareness.* For most of us, this process unfolds in stages. I will now try to show how it typically unfolds, as simply and clearly as possible.

Chapter 5
BECOMING AWARE

There is a fairly simple way to recognize what the PIG, APE and Ego are up to, and that is to recognize it after the fact. We can reflect on what we've just done, or what we did last night, and say: *Yep, that was my APE acting out again, protecting my Ego.*

This reflection after the fact is the sort of thing some religious people do when they "examine their conscience," and what twelve-steppers do when they "take inventory" of their behavior. At the very least we can now go back and try to clean up any messes we've made. And over time, we may learn the acting-out patterns of our PIG and our APE so well that sometimes we can see them coming and tame them before they act on our behalf.

When this occurs for you, you are beginning to "know yourself," as Socrates urged, in a most useful way. Not only in the intellectual sense of "yes, I know my strengths and the areas where I need improvement," but in the sense of being *aware* of yourself — on the fly, in so-called real time.

You are now learning to "watch" your inner creatures. And by the way, although we tend to use visual metaphors to speak of awareness and knowledge — keeping one's eyes wide open, seeing the light, and so forth — this doesn't mean you need to confine yourself to "watching" with your visual sense. You can use all the senses. Feel the PIG and APE stirring; listen for the voice of the Ego. You might even be able to "smell" the creatures doing something fishy or learn the taste of what it's like to be run by these creatures. Moreover you can use your sixth sense, intuition or mental awareness, to detect what's going on inside.

With this sort of introspection you begin to get the hang of awareness on all fronts. You will find, furthermore, that it enables you to un-learn the conditioning of the past, which has made you used to letting the inner creatures run your life. You can *practice* these things.

And practicing being aware of one's inner creatures has an added benefit. This practice, alone, can take you all the way to the highest level of awareness that we'll be talking about shortly — the level of pure knowing and presence, which goes beyond thinking, sensual perception, emotion or any other such mind-engaged activity.

Do you then leave those annoying creatures behind, once and for all? No, of course not. They'll always be there, and they are even helpful under certain circumstances. The difference is that they no longer have such a grip on you, because you *know* them. They may still get away with their mischief occasionally, just not very often and not for very long. There may be times, for instance, when you suddenly notice that you're not "being yourself" — that is, your highest and true self — which is a sign that your Ego has slipped back into the control room, and it's working the spell that makes you act wacky like a guy who turns into a werewolf, sprouting fangs and claws.

The difference is, you are no longer trapped in the state of Ego delusion. As you become highly aware, your Ego can actually become a good and useful thing to you, because it's something you *learn* from. Just being aware of your Ego can itself be a vehicle to enlightenment and lasting fulfillment.

But let's not get ahead of ourselves. Learning to recognize the inner creatures and reflecting upon the damage they can do is the place to start. To help with the task, there are "learning stories" in the back of this book that describe a number of the most typical patterns of inner-creature misbehavior — the types of PIG-ish and APE-ish blunders and Ego delusions that commonly plague many of us, in various life situations.

Through such learning we move to new levels of mental activity. The typical journey is a progression through three levels, from the most primitive to the highest. As you will see, it's a journey that grows more marvelous as we go along.

Starting to Become Aware: From Level 1 to Level 2

At the lowest level we are far from being able to separate ourselves from our Egos, or to detect the subtle tricks that our minds can play. We are not even aware of the extent to which we're being driven by our animal natures. So the first step forward is learning to keep the PIG and APE on the radar, and it looks like this:

Unaware —> Semi-Aware

When we are ignorant of the PIG and the APE we're at their mercy. Ironically, the primitive nature of these mind-creatures makes it easy for them to get the best of us. Since they work by automatic instinct, they work *fast* and they pay back in predictable, quick rewards. While this may be useful in certain instances, it accounts for a lot of those head-slap moments after we've done something foolish, when we ask: *What was I thinking?* Often the answer is: *"I" wasn't really "thinking" at all. The animal instincts jumped in; they usurped the function of thinking.* If we remain unaware that this is what's really happening, we'll remain stuck at the lowest level of functioning.

Moving up to the next level is partly a matter of adding time into the equation. If we can only slow down our reactions a little — delaying the drive for instant gratification, delaying the drive to avoid pain, maybe not always but sometimes — the delay will allow us some windows of time in which to deliberate. It will also allow us to look farther ahead along the time scale, taking a bigger-picture view of things than the PIG and the APE do. *If I blow off my obnoxious neighbor today, will that make it easier or harder living next to him for the rest of the year? If I jump on this job offer, I'll get more base pay ... but what will they expect from me for the money, and how will all the factors add up compared to staying where I am?*

No rocket science required here, my friends. What we're doing at this next level is merely what we call using our heads. To be more precise, this level is "mind-engaged." We're engaging our thinking minds and using them to take a rational view and a longer-term view.

The process consists of starting with some facts or assumptions we're pretty sure of — such as, "people don't like to be blown off" — then building from there. And the mind is good at that. The mind is analytical; it's made for reason and logic. Just "putting your mind to it" will take you a long way beyond running thoughtlessly unaware.

But there is a pitfall in staying at this level. Remember, the mind constructed the Ego, and the mind is involved in generating those emotions that "carry us away" — all of which can lead to behavior we'd have to agree is pretty darn "irrational" or "unreasonable." There are times when that mind seems to have a mind of its own. When my own mind acts up this way, it reminds me of the scenes in Stanley Kubrick's film *2001: A Space Odyssey* in which the onboard computer, a machine called HAL, takes over the spaceship and starts messing up the mission.

In fact, if we examine closely what the mind is doing in such moments, we'll usually find that it is engaged in something very insidious. It is using its powers of reason and logic to justify what the PIG and the APE are doing, or to justify what the Ego wants. We make decisions emotionally and then rationalize them intellectually.

That's why our foolish behavior can sometimes deeply perplex us. *Okay, maybe what I did was driven by blind instinct, or by this Ego thing. But it seemed so right; I thought it made perfect sense.* If we let it, the mind will then go on justifying and explaining its bad behavior after the fact — when it's not busy rehearsing and pre-justifying what it's about to do next. Sad to say, these often seem to be the main uses to which reason and logic are put.

I call the second level "Semi-Aware" because it is ruled by the thinking mind, which is limited; the powers of reason and logic are limited.

For further evidence of the limits, you may have noticed that sometimes we have trouble forcing ourselves to do what seems rational — such as sticking to a diet, instead of running out at midnight for a half-gallon of ice cream. Or, when it comes to dealing with other people, surely you've noticed that they won't always "listen to reason" *as your mind has concocted it.* Therefore, we'll want to move beyond the limited perspective of the mind-engaged level.

As Albert Einstein said, "The significant problems we face cannot be solved at the same level of thinking at which we created them." Or to put it another way: "Pure logic is the ruin of the spirit." I found that inside a fortune cookie. Later I learned it is a quotation from Antoine de Saint-Exupery, and it's the one that did it for me. Having been trained as an engineer, I had believed that if anything could not be explained by logic, it wasn't real.

As we move to the third and highest level — the level beyond the thinking mind — the very manner in which I am talking to you will have to change. If you have been reading carefully, you'll have noticed that just about everything I've said to this point is, itself, on the mind-engaged level of thinking, reasoning, and logic. A lot of what comes next will sound mystical. Which it is.

From Level 2 to Level 3: The Mystical Nature of Awareness

Moving to the third level looks like this:

Unaware —> Semi-Aware —> Aware

And it's hard to define this level. Words themselves break down, either taking on multiple meanings or failing to capture the intended meaning. I can call the awareness that exists at this level Awareness with a capital A, to signify how "big" or "full" it is, if that helps ... but words can only allude to it.

The realm we are now in is slippery for the rational thinking mind. Just the approach to it is slippery. You may recall that at previous points, sometimes I've spoken of "the mind" thinking and acting, and sometimes I've spoken of "you" or "I" doing such things. As if there were a "you" or an "I" that can operate *separately* from the mind. Or above it, or beyond it. Or something like that.

How could this be possible? Is there a sort of super-you who is outside the mind, or different from the mind ... and is something more?

Yes.

There is a larger you which is more than just a thinker. It is a *knower*.

Let's call this knower the "big YOU." And call the mind, the thinker, the "little you." They're both part of You, the person who lives in this world (with a capital Y up front, as in Your Name).

Now we come to the heart of the human predicament. Often, we don't know that we have a knower. We've come to rely so much on thinking that for the most part, our knower is hidden. Big YOU, the knower, is obscured by little you, the thinker. I call this the YOU-you obstruction.

In this obstructed state, we may get some glimmers of the big YOU, but it's overshadowed by our constant thinking.

In the light of Awareness, the different facets of ourselves are revealed and emerge distinctly.

And, we can add some words to try and make clearer the distinction between the little you and the big YOU, as shown on the next page.

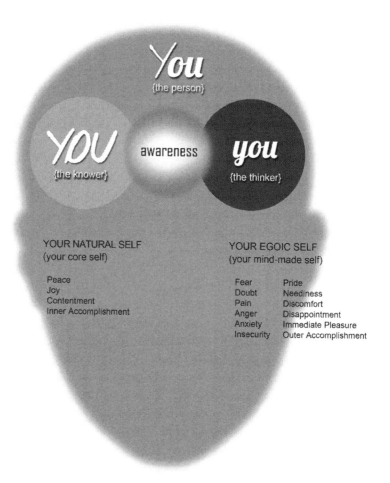

YOU
{the person}

YOU {the knower}   awareness   **you** {the thinker}

YOUR NATURAL SELF
(your core self)

Peace
Joy
Contentment
Inner Accomplishment

YOUR EGOIC SELF
(your mind-made self)

Fear   Pride
Doubt   Neediness
Pain   Discomfort
Anger   Disappointment
Anxiety   Immediate Pleasure
Insecurity   Outer Accomplishment

WITNESSING THE EGOIC MIND

Little you, the thinker, is that same old mind that we've been talking about — the creator of the made-up self, the Ego, and thus as long as it remains coupled with the Ego we call it the Egoic mind. The little you gets a lot done in this thinking world of ours. It's a mover and shaker, a struggler and a juggler. But if we get stuck in it, it's a shaking, quaking prison.

That's what the poet William Blake was describing when he wrote about the "mind-forged manacles," and the "dark Satanic mills" — which, contrary to the popular opinion of thinking minds, were not factories. They were the mills of logic and reason that can grind our souls to dust. Blake was also referring to the mental prison when he wrote that "man has closed himself up, till he sees all things through narrow chinks of his cavern."

A little harsh? Maybe not. Under little you, the thinker, in our picture, are listed just a few of the horde of obsessions that fill the space inside the mind-cave. When you remain locked in there, you are breathing these obsessions; you are swarmed and fogged by them. Anything you're able to see in the narrow views through your narrow chinks is clouded by them. *You don't even know who you are.*

Awareness lifts you out, to a place where you can breathe cleanly. And now, here and now, there is no doubt about it. You *know* who is what. Big YOU, the knower, is your core natural being. The view is happier from here. Profoundly happy, without the shaking and quaking, the struggling and juggling.

Is big YOU, the core being, solid like a rock? Well, it's solid like a firm foundation that won't go away, once you stand in it. But a very significant quality is that it's not dense. It is not a prison; it won't obscure anything; it can reveal everything and the light of Awareness shines through it. Big YOU, your natural being, is *open*.

Big YOU is capable of being intimately aware of people and events in the surrounding world, so intimately as to be connected with them, and even identify with them — not in the delusional

Ego sense of "owning" them, but in the sense of being one with them.

Another word for Awareness is *presence*. Presence is the way out of the prison, or as my daughter says, "Presence is the key to all locked doors." Presence simply means being where you are, and being *when* you are — not mired in thinking about the past, trying to grind it to analytic dust; and not living in a fantasized future either, just being present and aware now.

It's all right there — or actually, right "then" — in the moment called now. What is now, if not the product of the past, and where — when? — are the seeds of the future if not now? Eckhart Tolle was pointing to this, and much more, when he wrote "The Power of Now." When else would you find any power whatsoever?

To be frankly mystical, your natural being is intimately aware of, and connected with, the life force of the universe. That's what makes it the "big" YOU. It's the YOU that is never alone, the YOU through which everything runs. And that's how you can know more than you think.

Decoupling the Mind from the Ego

Now there is one more step. You may get the impression that I'm saying the mind is a villain, and thinking is bad for you. That would be incorrect. Of course the human mind is a wonderful instrument, but please note the choice of the word. *Instrument.* An instrument is something to be played, and used, for high purposes, like a musical instrument — the mind is an organ! — or like a scientific instrument, of which the mind is by far the most marvelous. Some say it is our sixth sense organ.

When used well, this thinking instrument, this organ, can do great things. The important question is, who or what is doing the using?

Ideally the big YOU, the core self, is using the mind. This is the "natural" state of affairs — or put another way, it's the "state of mind" that is in harmony with nature. The big YOU, with its transcendent connectedness, receives "inspirations" from a larger intelligence, and, as it were, transmits them to the mind to be put into forms: words, music, human creations and expressions of all kinds. The way I like to describe this process for myself is by saying, "My core self asks my mind to do projects for it." When this is happening, that is a happy and fruitful condition to be in.

However, that condition can only exist if the mind is *available* to the big YOU. And there are times when it isn't available. Those are the times when the mind is all tied up with, entangled with, the Ego. It's almost like a bad love affair or a conspiracy. The mind, always busy on its own, has created a false identity — the Ego — and falls in love with it. The Ego reciprocates: it feels right at home in this affair, and why shouldn't it?

This is an *incestuous* conspiracy, and it can lead to further outrage. With the mind and the Ego in collusion, they're always going to be cooking up intrigues. They'll always be wanting to usurp the rightful functions of the big YOU and put the Ego on the throne; they'll be hatching plots that lead to madness and misery. That is the kind of thinking that's bad and it's a mean and sorry state of mind: the Egoic mind. Unfortunately it is the state in which many of us live, much of the time.

To make the mind available, it literally has to be de-coupled from its incestuous dalliance with the Ego.

Now the mind can be used as the instrument it was meant to be. And what will bring about the decoupling? Again, Awareness is all it takes. Who would cheat when they're being watched? Certainly not the mind; it's too smart for that. As soon as it knows that YOU know what's up, it will decouple itself from the Ego and assume its place.

* * *

None of this should be taken as the absolute "truth." We have just been using words to try to signify levels beyond words. The following chapters will bring all of the levels, including the esoteric, back to the practical.

Chapter 6
WHAT'S DRIVING YOU?

One of the most popular personal growth programs in my younger days was the Est training, developed by Werner Erhard. Est was always controversial. Some people considered it a scary cult, while others found it valuable. The story I want to pass along to you is meant to be neither a criticism or an endorsement of the program. I am using the story to make a specific point, as you shall soon see.

A man I know, let's call him Mike, took the Est training when he was about thirty. Mike is very intelligent. He was doing well in a career that defeats many people who try it. But his personal life was in chaos and so were his thoughts and feelings, much of the time, when he wasn't focused on his work. He had tried reading about Zen Buddhism and other approaches that he thought might help him "manage his energies" — and therefore manage his life — but he never seemed able to apply what he had read. So he signed up for Est, and here is the story in his own words:

The training was in a room at a convention center, with about a hundred people sitting in chairs and the trainer up front. We were in there for two solid weekends. After the first weekend, I was telling my friends that the experience was worth it for the entertainment value alone. Our trainer was the real high-energy, in-your-face type. He came in cracking jokes and telling us, right off the bat, how screwed up we all were: "Your life doesn't work. That's why you're here. And you expect me to fix it for you — ha! Ha ha ha!" That kind of thing.

But the best part was when people stood up to answer questions or make comments. It was like the human comedy on parade, just an ongoing display of all of the crazy justifications and misinterpretations that people use to explain themselves. You knew the trainer was going to poke a hole in each person's bubble, and after a while, he could do it without even talking. He'd just roll his eyes or have this "Oh, really?" expression on his face, and everybody would roar.

And wouldn't you know, some of these people actually looked as if they suddenly realized the stupidity of whatever they were saying. They'd sort of blush and chuckle and say "Oh, okay, I got it." I didn't stand up myself because I was having too much fun watching, and I figured I was learning things in the process.

Well. Day three, start of the second weekend. And surprise, surprise: a different trainer. This is Ken, and he's a quiet and scholarly type. Even wearing, would you believe it, a cardigan sweater.

No more fireworks. I was getting bored. Finally Ken says he's going to reveal some great paradox of existence to us — I forget exactly what it was — and he starts writing words and drawing diagrams all over the big whiteboard in the front of the room.

He wrote this one sentence and underlined it. Again, I can't remember exactly what it said, because of the shock that came after. It was something on the order of "The ultimate test of reality is what's real." So right away I put my hand up. I said "Ken, excuse me, wait a minute. Isn't that a tautology? Or, uh, some type of logical fallacy? I mean, it doesn't —"

And the way he cut me off was, he just put down his marker and he stood there, looking at me. Then he said very quietly and calmly: "Mike. We've been here for two and a half days now, talking about *your life*. And the first time you say anything is to say that maybe somebody made an error in logic?"

It took a few seconds for that to sink in. Then, when I saw what I'd been doing, I was absolutely mortified. Nobody laughed. It almost would've been easier if they had. But, that was my big aha moment. It didn't cure all my ills right away, but it definitely got me pointed to a path that's been more fruitful.

One could interpret this story by saying that up to that point, Mike had been "intellectualizing" the program. As he put it when he first told me the story, "It's a way of learning stuff but distancing yourself from it, so you don't have to do anything. There's comfort in that" — it's like being a spectator and not getting onto the field.

I would go a step deeper. In the terms we have been using, I would say that up to the aha moment, Mike was not actually present in the room. His big YOU, his natural self, was obscured. Only his Ego was engaged. It was his Ego that was doing the listening and watching. I would also suggest that previously, when he read the various books that didn't help much, perhaps they didn't help because his Ego was doing the reading.

Mike, by the way, agreed that this was a good description of his former state, once I had explained this book's terminology to him. The message of his story, which I will now try to flesh out more clearly, is backed up by my conversations and experiences with many other people as well.

The Paradox That Keeps Us Trapped

Presumably you are reading this book because you want it to lead to positive changes in your life. Unfortunately, a lot of people read personal-growth books and enroll in programs without seeing much in the way of results. In a few cases, the book is flawed or the program isn't appropriate for the person. However, one would think that if you tried a number of them, you would at least start making some significant progress. Yet many so-called enlightenment shoppers never come close to the light at the end of the tunnel. Is the whole enlightenment industry a scam? Unlikely.

It is far more likely that the person who can't seem to change for the better is trapped in a form of the old Catch-22 paradox, which goes like this:

➤ Personal growth is all about changing your thoughts and behaviors.

➤ For that to happen, what is *driving* your thoughts and behaviors has to change.

➤ But if what's driving you to pursue personal growth in the first place is some part of you that doesn't really want to change — if it's a part of you that is after something else instead — then you're not going to change.

Let's go back through this paradox using a couple of examples, to try to make it crystal clear.

When I say that what's "driving" your thoughts and behaviors has to change, this could include everything from your long-term goals in life to the impulses that drive moment-to-moment behavior. For instance:

Suppose one of your main goals in life is to make as much money as possible, and you have started getting unmistakable messages that your obsession with money is becoming unhealthy. Your friends are saying that it's all you seem to think or talk about. Your doctor warns you about the stress you're putting yourself under; your accountant warns you about playing fast and loose with the tax deductions you claim. Your partner complains that money means more to you than the relationship does.

We've all known people who were in a state like this, literally being consumed by the drive for something or other, if not money.

And what do such people typically do when they are warned that it's time to make changes? If they respond at all, they usually respond by making tweaks and adjustments, trying to bring their obsession "under control" or "back into balance."

So let us presume that's what you do about your obsession with money. You force yourself to take a vacation so you can relax a little, whether you feel like it or not. Maybe you stop at the bookstore to buy a couple of books other than the ones in the Money section, so you can read them and show your friends that you're able to talk about something else. Maybe you tell your partner that you really care, and to prove it, you make reservations at a fancy restaurant and buy a nice gift ... but wait a minute. You're still thinking and acting in terms of money, aren't you? Still driven by using money to prove a point and to show who you are.

People who follow such a path rarely change significantly or for very long, before they backslide. They remain attached to what has been driving them, largely unaware of the hold that it has on them.

The same is true of the moment-to-moment drives that take hold suddenly. If you are constantly driven by urges to lash out at people, or to satisfy sudden cravings, you'll be a slave to your impulses — to those chaotic "energies" that Mike used to have so much trouble trying to manage, in his life-is-a-mess days. Those energies of course are the same things we call the PIG, the APE and the Ego. When driven by the creatures, you may have a certain degree of success in life in terms of accomplishing things. But you probably won't find much peace or happiness unless and until you can reach a state where they're no longer driving your thoughts and behavior so much.

Now comes the heart of the paradox. You embark on a personal growth campaign — why? Maybe because life is painful and full of problems. Or maybe because it is just unsatisfying or perplexing; maybe something keeps telling you that there ought to be more to life, even if you're not sure what it is. So you become a seeker, in search of the answer to your problems or the whatever-it-is you ought to have.

And maybe you even "find" the answer! Maybe it's right there in a book or program. You get that thrill, that flood of exhilaration, that comes when your mind says "Case closed!" and lights up a victory cigar. Except, except ...

The days go by, the weeks and months go by, and nothing much improves in your life. The problems persist; the wacky thoughts and behavior are still there; the unsatisfied feeling has returned. Perhaps you had been going around telling people that you found the answer, and they are starting to make little remarks which indicate that it sure doesn't look like you found it. Or perhaps you have noticed that you didn't really get around to applying those great principles and techniques you learned — maybe because it was too much trouble, or they didn't seem to work, or they worked a little bit and then you forgot.

At any rate, there is only one answer ... and it's to look for another answer. Read another book, try another program. Back to square one. Brainwash, rinse, repeat ...

What happened?

If I were a betting person I would bet that such a person has been trapped, all along, in the Egoic mind. The Ego doesn't want to change. It wants a different kind of reward. The Ego wants *answers.*

The Ego is uncomfortable with, even fearful of, the unknown. It suspects there is some fishy thing out there that is causing problems and needs to be identified — or maybe it just worries that it will be scorned or ridiculed if other smart Egos notice that it doesn't know what every smart Ego ought to know.

The Ego also wants praise and recognition for finding answers, and for being able to tell other people what the answer is. That's how you get an A on the test, a gold star on your forehead.

So. If the Ego is driving the pursuit of personal growth in the first place — or driving it to a large extent — then you're stuck. The Ego will stop as soon as it gets the answer. It certainly doesn't want the answer to be "applied" in any way that might undermine its rule. Besides, why bother with the application? Mission accomplished! The answer has been found and brought into the mind-cave where the Ego can have it, to revel in it and to put it on the shelf for display. Until the thrill wears off, or the answer turns out to be not enough, or not the right one, or last year's answer that is oh, so *over* ... and it's time to go out and get another.

The Hungry Mouth

The Ego is always craving, never satisfied. Some of us persuade ourselves that this is a good thing. We say we have inquiring minds, always thirsting for new knowledge like the great thinkers of history. And in a certain condition, this is indeed a good thing, but the condition is as follows. It's a good thing if — as we saw in the last chapter — the big YOU, the core self, is engaged and in charge, using the mind as a wonderful tool. In that case, by all means let's keep stocking the mental toolroom with new pieces of knowledge; they're likely to be useful.

However if the Ego is in charge, and has hijacked the mind, its creator, to its own purposes, then the result will not be so good. In fact, if the desired result is personal change and growth, that result won't come at all. The result will just be an Ego-feeding.

We've seen that the Ego isn't really us, that it is a made-up version of ourselves we carry around with us. Imagine this Ego, this shadow self, standing next to you. Now here is a bit of knowledge or wisdom that looks tasty. The hungry Ego standing next to you says, "I want it." And there it goes: the Ego puts it into its mouth and swallows it. Now here's another, and another, and the Ego gobbles them up, too.

You can't get nourishment by putting food into an imaginary mouth. It drops into a bottomless pit. When you're feeding the wrong mouth — feeding a fake, a phantom — you'll always be hungry. And that is the case with the perpetual seekers who never seem to find what they need. Every nugget they come across gets dropped into a vanishing bag.

The 'Yes, But' and 'The Story'

Interestingly, the problem of never being able to change can also be found in some people who, at first glance, seem to be quite different from perpetual seekers. In fact they seem to be the exact opposites of seekers. They're the "Yes, but" people.

In Eric Berne's classic book *Games People Play,* one of the big self-defeating games is called "Yes, But." Somebody has a dreadful problem she can't solve. You keep suggesting obvious solutions, but to no avail, because for every solution she has a reason it won't work or it can't be done: "Yes, but ..."

I met a couple of Yes, but people in the course of writing this chapter. One was a young man who had earned a very nice college degree but couldn't find a job in his field, not even an entry-level job. The other was an older woman who'd been wanting for years to move out of the city she hated living in, but never moved.

It was agonizing to be with these people. First I had to listen to their stories, their tales of woe. Then of course I started asking why they didn't try this or that, only to be met at every turn with explanations of why it was impossible. Some of their explanations were longer and more convoluted than the original tales. The only bright spot was knowing that once I left their company, my agony would end, while these people, unfortunately, would go on living theirs.

The yes-butters come across as different from perpetual seekers in the sense that they don't appear to be seeking answers at all. On the contrary, they are resisting answers. But at bottom, it's the same difficulty: the Ego is in charge, driving thoughts and behavior.

Just as the Ego likes to look for answers, it also likes to look for reasons. What the Ego seeks in these cases is to fortify its current state — and thus, its very existence. It seeks justification, and sympathy, for lack of accomplishment despite being an individual of such high merit and noble character. It seeks to be listened to.

It is creating a *story* to explain itself. And the story, like the Ego itself, is not to be threatened.

If I live in my Ego, I believe that the story is a true representation of me. And therefore I will go on telling that story. The PIG and the APE, being servants of the Ego, perform their services here. Any time my PIG spots a willing listener, or an opportunity to bring up the story in the course of conversation, it will nudge my Ego in the mental ribs and say, *There's your cue, you're on!* If my Ego is reading a book or article, and sees a quotation that backs up my story, the PIG will squeal with delight: *Ooh, we can use that. It feels sooo good! Let's memorize it and try it out on some people today!*

Of course the APE, the avoider of painful experiences, plays the role of protector. If a listener starts to question the story, the APE's job is to cue the Yes-buts. If a book or article starts looking as if it's going to contradict my story, or worse yet expose the story for the sham that it is, the APE will start to whisper: *This is nonsense. Put the thing down.* And if that fails — if something compels me to go on reading — the APE may pull out his ultimate stop-the-reading trick: *You are getting sleepy. Verrry sleepy ...*

One of the things that made the Est training controversial was the rule about staying in the training room at all times, except when a break was announced. This was known among critics of Est as the "You're not allowed to go the bathroom" rule. In fact, people were able to excuse themselves to use the toilet if they insisted, but they were strongly discouraged from doing so — for the same reason they were warned that they would be awakened if they nodded off while sitting in the training room. Falling asleep and "needing" to leave the room were well known to be avoidance mechanisms, i.e. APE tricks. People were liable to resort to them if a part of the program came along that they actually did "need" to hear, but didn't want to hear — i.e., anything that might undermine their stories, their Egos.

Naturally we do such things unaware of what's really driving us. People who duck out of a personal-growth program at a crucial time will say, "Hey, it's not some avoidance mechanism telling me to go. It's my bladder." They feel quite certain that a primal, physical need is what's giving them the urge to go. But of course it feels that way, because the APE is part of our primitive limbic system, and therefore whatever the APE is urging us to do may be expressed as a physical urge ... whether it's a sudden need to urinate, or an overwhelming need to sleep.

Moreover, the Egoic mind will help to keep us in a state of denial, by thinking up justifications and rationalizations for our little avoidance tricks. When we stop reading a book or fail to heed its advice, we typically won't have an inkling that the Ego or the Ego's story might have been threatened. If anything, the mind will add to our story, with a story about why the book didn't work for us.

It's dizzying. Paradoxes usually are. The point is simply this. If we truly want to change and grow, as opposed to reading about change and growth, the first "practical" stage is just to *be keenly aware of what's driving us.*

The Gift of Awareness

That stage alone, being aware of what drives our thoughts and behavior, can take us a long way. Some thoughts and behaviors may even begin to change on their own. You may "naturally" start to feel happier, or make clearer choices, without much additional effort.

As you practice awareness, you will know what you need to do. It will come to you. That is the gift of awareness.

There will probably still be a need to keep learning practical approaches for particular situations. We'll address these in chapters to come. But awareness of what drives us has to come first, and it is not a trivial stage, for several reasons.

As we've seen, what drives us is often not obvious or easy to detect. It is a covert operation. And just as covert operations in a war can foul up the best-laid battle plans if they go undetected, covert operations inside the head can foul up the best-laid plans or recipes for personal growth.

Also, it's easy to confuse "awareness" with "analysis," which can become a major side-track if we proceed from there into over-analysis. The idea that we need to be aware of what drives us isn't new. Entire schools of psychotherapy are based on this idea. For some people, they work. I am suggesting, however, that for many of us there isn't really a need to delve deeply into such matters as which parent we're trying to prove wrong, or how our money drive is associated with our sex drive.

I'm giving you only three creatures to watch — easy to remember, no need to write them down. And I am suggesting that above all you watch the Ego, it being the thief within the household that is most likely to steal the silverware.

But what keeps the watcher's job from being supremely easy is that there aren't many clear-cut, simple rules of thumb for monitoring the inner creatures. For instance, given what we've learned so far about the PIG, it may be tempting to think: *Oh, instant gratification is bad. Therefore, any time I feel the urge for instant gratification, I should ignore it or fight it because that's my bad PIG acting up.*

There are a couple of problems with this. One is, I am not advising you to fight your inner drives. That's usually a losing battle. Just practice becoming aware of them instead of playing mind-games with your own mind — which, almost by definition, are games you can't win.

Furthermore, instant gratification is not always harmful. Nor is it always harmful to act quickly to avoid painful experiences! Remember, the PIG and APE are survival instincts. There are times when they can help us survive. The trouble is, often we are so shockingly *unaware* of our inner drives that we can't even tell when the creatures are afoot, let alone make a distinction like the one between "good APE" and "bad APE."

And this is perhaps the greatest difficulty. When we set out to learn and practice awareness of what drives us, we may be starting from a much lower state than we suspect. Much of the time, in fact, we are unaware of how unaware we are. Let's look at some evidence.

Into the Maze of Everyday Unawareness

Here is a typical example. It's a hot day. Really hot, and you're out in it — maybe taking a long walk or a run, or working on something around the house. You are starting to feel unusually weak-limbed and drained. Suddenly your thinking mind remembers the scary alerts that it's heard on the TV news, and you begin to worry: could this be heat exhaustion? Sunstroke? Or the onset of an actual stroke?

Chances are, the problem is simpler than that. Much simpler. *You need a drink of water!* Somehow, in our sheltered and yet oh-so-busy modern lives, many of us have become inattentive to this basic survival need. It's gotten to the point where health authorities have to remind us to stay "hydrated." Some of us then follow the advice to an extreme that borders on the ridiculous, not even venturing out for a short jog in the park without carrying a two-pound bottle of liquid — despite the fact that there are water fountains all around — while others let their minds get preoccupied while they run or work in the garden, and ignore the call of thirst that begins long before their legs turn rubbery.

This illustrates how unaware of the inner PIG we can be. We'll remain oblivious to it when it is urging us to do something healthy ... and then let ourselves be run by the same PIG just a little later, when it wants to "reward" us for our hard work in the heat by stuffing us full of ice cream, pitchers of beer, or whatever.

The same sort of thing can happen with the APE. One of its survival-instinct jobs, from back in primitive times, is to help us avoid confrontations with other animals that might be dangerous. Yet there are times when it appears that this basic function goes utterly undone.

You're driving somewhere in a hurry. The driver ahead of you is painfully slow and erratic, sometimes almost stopping at green lights, probably lost in an unfamiliar part of town. No sympathy from you, though. You lean on the horn: *honk honk honnnk!* You wave and gesture angrily, to make sure he'll see in his rear-view mirror that you are telling him how stupid he is. Isn't that more than discourteous? Isn't that a little dangerous? What if the driver is a big guy who pulls over at the next light, climbs out, and comes after you?

Or, what if that slow driver you've been honking and shaking your fist at turns out to be going to the same important event you are? What if the vehicle parks there, right in front of yours, and he or she steps out and it's the guest of honor you were hoping to meet and impress? This is exactly what happened to a friend of mine once. He said the driver who stepped out of the big, black, shiny SUV was an elegantly dressed woman, clutching a beaded evening bag and glaring at him "as if she thought my next move would be to snatch her purse."

Talk about a painful experience. Now, why doesn't the APE help us avoid this risky road-rage stuff? One reason might be that the APE, conditioned to avoid immediate pain and danger, just doesn't look far enough ahead to possible consequences like those my friend suffered.

But here's the likely bottom-line reason. In cases like my friend's, the PIG has priority to take control. The PIG will try to throw all the energy you've got into getting there in a hurry, even regardless of physical dangers such as crashing the car, because the PIG is serving its *most* potent master: not physical safety, but the Ego.

The Ego doesn't want to be late for an important date. The Ego wants to get there early, walk in looking good, and have a chance to network with the VIPs. The slow driver in front is a threat to that. So if the APE is going to do anything, it's going to answer the master's call as well, and jump right in there beside the PIG to go: *Honk honk, blankety-blank, get out of the way!* In fact, that's probably why road rage is so powerful and can be so hard to resist. It's a product of the PIG and APE ganging up in service of the Ego.

So here is a useful distinction, or rule of thumb if you will:

The APE itself, like the PIG, is neither good nor bad. It might be trying to perform a healthy service. But when the APE or PIG is serving the Ego, that's almost always trouble.

And here is a further illustration of that rule. Many people who let their PIGs lure them into trouble will turn around and shoot themselves in the other foot as well. They'll let the APE prevent them from doing useful things that aren't dangerous at all, and need not be painful.

For instance, what do you think is the most common phobia in our society? A number of surveys have shown that it isn't the fear of heights, which at least can do you some good if it keeps you from taking foolish chances on roofs and ladders. Nor is it the fear of death in general, which can be a problem if it's obsessive but seems an understandable fear to have. These fears rank high but they don't top the chart. What more people fear, more than anything else, is speaking in front of an audience.

In his book *Lost in the Cosmos,* an inquiry into the weirdness of human nature, the writer Walker Percy found this fact to be one of the weirdest. After all, he wrote, "A wolf howling alone in a wolf pack doesn't get stage fright." So why should your average human be terrified of speaking to a group of his or her fellow humans? Percy gave a list of possible explanations, some of them tongue-in-cheek but nonetheless close to the mark, like this:

Is it because you fear a total failure of performance such as never happened before in the history of the world, so that not one word will come to your mind and world chaos will follow?

And here was the one at the end of the list:

Is it because you know that what you present to the world is a persona, a mask, that it is a very fragile disguise, that God alone knows what is underneath since you clearly do not ... and that if the persona fails, what is revealed is unspeakable (literally, because you can't speak it) ...?

If this sounds familiar, it should. All of what is said here can easily be translated into the terms that we've been using. The APE wants to stop us from speaking in front of groups — even small groups, as in a classroom or a business meeting — because its main task is to protect the Ego, and these events put the Ego at risk.

If your Ego, the identity that your mind has made up for you, is that of a person who knows what she's doing, then messing up even a small speech would threaten that identity by showing that maybe you don't. Or if your mind-made identity is that of a person who's actually rather clueless, then messing up will only confirm it, while ruining the image of a person who at least knows when to keep her mouth shut. Either way, the result could throw *your* mind-constructed world into chaos, so the APE says: *better not try it.*

And ironically, the greatest fear is that the "disguise," the Ego, will slip out of place entirely. In that case, what might be "revealed" is your core being — which, as Walker Percy noted and as the previous chapter of this book explained, is indeed a being beyond the realm of logic and words, inexplicable and literally "unspeakable."

But how sad it is that so many of us are afraid to reveal the natural self! Think of how liberating it could be to speak from the big YOU, instead of from some made-up version of the little you. And it is eminently possible to do so, for while the big YOU may be "unspeakable" in the sense that *words can't describe its essence,* it won't leave you speechless in front of a crowd, in the sense of not knowing what to say about a particular subject.

Quite the opposite! Once you are able to acknowledge the big YOU, once you are able to trust it — knowing that it is beyond the control of the Egoic thinking mind, but connected to a larger intelligence — very often it will lead you to say what really needs to be said. You are in a state where you're able to "speak from the heart" instead of merely "speaking your mind." You'll have people coming up to you afterward with comments like "I was thinking the same thing, but I didn't know how to say it," or "Thanks for raising that question; I was afraid to ask it."

However, we can't get to that state when the Ego is in the way and the APE is scrambling to protect the Ego. Neither can we get there when the PIG is pushing forward to feed the Ego, which happens to be the source of many annoying speeches. Have you been at, say, a public meeting where someone in the audience stands up to speak his mind, and it turns into a long-winded harangue on some side issue that doesn't seem related to the subject at hand? His Ego, his mind-made identity, is probably tied into what it knows or thinks it knows about that side issue, and the impulsive PIG couldn't resist the opportunity to show off. The result is a guy on the path to wearing out many welcomes.

Myths About Motivation

Now let's bust some myths. Our inner drives are also sometimes called motives or motivations, which leads to another source of confusion, as there are so many misconceptions floating around on the subject of "motivation."

In every perplexing case we have looked at so far, from not knowing how to take care of ourselves on a hot day to getting tied in knots about speaking in public, I would propose that the underlying problem is one of motivation.

However, by that I don't mean a *lack* of motivation. There are so-called motivational speakers who give the impression that all we have to do is "get motivated" and we can make all our dreams come true, living happily ever after. This seems absurd.

For one thing, some highly motivated people are delusional. They will work away for years at an invention, or a relationship, that hasn't got a chance. Also, modern history is filled with the stories of highly motivated people with names like Hitler and McCarthy, who did make their dreams come true — but only for a short while, at a terrible price to others, and the dreamers themselves ended in misery.

Highly motivated misery isn't a rare condition. You can find examples in your own neighborhood. They're the people who chase success at any cost: they may be making lots of money and their kids may get good grades in school, but you wouldn't enjoy living in their household. Just as virtue is its own reward, crazy motivation is its own punishment. *When you're running on the wrong fuel, it pollutes your insides.*

Besides, very few of us actually lack motivation. Do you know anyone who has no wants or desires? If so, the person is likely to be clinically depressed, and needs expert help. Typically we're at the other end of the scale, wanting more than we could ever fit into our lives. Steven Wright, the comedian, summed up the predicament neatly: "You can't have everything. Where would you put it?" Usually we realize this. But from there, we often jump to a broad conclusion that is sort of half-true and half myth.

We may conclude that the trick is to "focus" or "channel" our motivational energies — letting some things go, setting a few priorities, and following through on them. As far as it goes, that's a sound guiding principle. We don't want to over-extend ourselves and burn out, or putter through life having many goals and achieving none. And certainly there will be times when we have to choose one pursuit over another. You can marry Harry or Larry, but in most modern societies, not both at once.

Now, however, let's consider where this guiding principle falls short. First, we can be misled into thinking we have to sacrifice some aspect of our lives in order to fulfill another. Women used to be told they could have a career or a family but not both. Today, while it isn't easy, many women find a way. *Not all choices in life are either-or.* If a boy says he'd like to grow up to be a brain surgeon or a lion tamer, the temptation is to smile and say "Well, you'd better pick one." In fact, the kid is voicing the passionate interests that motivate him, and by being creative he may find a way to combine those passions. He could become a veterinarian, or a scientist studying how animals think — or something else beyond the either-or choice, something that you and I can't imagine, because we haven't done it.

The line of thinking that says "It's all about focus" has deeper flaws as well. It assumes, for instance, that we know what we "really want" in life. For many of us, this seems to be a primary point of confusion in itself.

And going deeper yet: It is hard to focus on the grand, life-trajectory kinds of priorities — or even to be clear on what they are — if we have trouble finding clarity in the moment. The road to happiness doesn't just start right now, it's *always* right now, and if our state in many of our right-nows is a state of being tugged here and there by forces we don't understand, it's likely to be a rough ride.

Which brings us back to the basics of motivation. At any given moment we are liable to have all sorts of motivations. The PIG, the APE and the Ego will see to that. They are busy, busy creatures. And good luck using "will power" to try and discipline these creatures into sitting quietly in a corner like tamed lions. They'll take a bite when you least expect it.

To reiterate: what's needed is *awareness* and the ability to make *distinctions*. To begin noticing where various drives or motivations come from ... and to begin recognizing which are healthy and which are not-so-healthy or downright unhealthy.

Conspiracies

Speaking of which, here is another important distinction. We have seen that the PIG and the APE on their own are not necessarily troublesome, but either one in service of the Ego usually is. And furthermore:

> When the PIG and the APE are in action *together,* serving the Ego, it is *always* trouble and usually trouble of the worst kind.

Now you have a full-fledged conspiracy of creatures, a feeding frenzy. The Ego and its minions are getting rewarded in multiple ways, and in mutually reinforcing ways. This conspiracy drives patterns of thought and behavior that are very seductive — often the hardest to resist, and hard to break out of once you let them take hold.

Let's look at a couple of examples. These little scenarios show the difference between isolated acts of instant gratification that are mostly harmless, or even healthy, and conspiracies that are anything but.

You are sitting at home in the evening with nothing in particular on the schedule. Suddenly the thought comes: hmm, I haven't talked to my friend Leslie in a while. Why not give her a call right now? You'll enjoy it — Leslie is the kind of person who is so free-flowing that before you know it, you're talking and laughing about everything imaginable — and, by calling, you'll help to keep the friendship alive. You will be spending some time, but tonight is one of those rare nights when there is time to spare; the phone call may be the best possible use of it.

Here we have instant gratification that can be fulfilling, with no harm done. Better yet, along with the instant rewards you get longer-term benefits too. Quite a bargain!

But those types of scenes don't always work out so cleanly. Sometimes they look more like this:

You are sitting in front of your computer on a workday, staring at a piece of work you've been struggling with, when who should come to mind? Old friend Leslie, of course. Why not check your email to see if she's written? Or your Facebook page? Why not send her a note — and while you're on the Internet, check the news and the sports, to be sure you're well informed? And then, maybe you'll see a Facebook post or a news column that brings up a subject you have strong opinions about. Wouldn't this be a good time to put those opinions into writing, and post them under "Comments" for the world to see?

Of course, what you're doing now is called procrastination. It's also a classic case of being driven by a conspiracy. Your PIG feeds the Ego by pursuing the little instant gratifications that can be gotten much more quickly and easily than the big satisfaction of finishing that tough job — while at the same time, your APE avoids the painful experience of tackling whatever has to be tackled to finish it. Very seductive, very powerful, hard to break out of. That's why procrastination is one of the most common bad habits and, apparently, has been for centuries.

Another familiar case:

Winter has begun. You've been thinking that you would enjoy having a nice, long woolen scarf. Then one day while strolling through a department store you see a rack of beautiful scarves, on sale at half price. You might as well buy one. Granted, it's a little bit of a so-called "ego trip," because you want a long scarf for the look, not only for the warmth. But this is a small item, easily within your budget, and it's going to give you pleasure every day. You may not find a good selection at such a low price again, so it makes sense to buy now.

So far, so good. But what happens next?

You have bought the scarf. It's already draped around your shoulders, with the sales receipt in your pocket. And you feel elated, almost ecstatic. You are experiencing what some call a shopper's rush, but what is in fact the PIG feeding the Ego in multiple ways. To begin with, yes, you're looking good! You've been checking yourself out in every mirror in the store. You also feel the elation of having gotten a good deal — you're a smart investor, like Warren Buffett — plus the elation that comes with *making a choice and getting the results instantly.* Experts say this is often a key element in compulsive shopping. People feel powerless and ineffective, so they go out and shop. It's a way of wielding instant influence in the material world.

It's not at all unusual to succumb to that feeding of the Ego by making one more impulse purchase, or two more. Maybe you're able to stop after that and say "Time to go home." But watch out, because now the APE is sneaking into the picture as well. If you're one of those people who shop, in part, to make up for feelings of powerlessness elsewhere in life, you are probably avoiding some painful issues that need to be confronted. If it gets to the point where you are spending time in the mall that really ought to be spent doing other things, maybe things that would put the Ego at risk, that's unmistakably the APE. And now the conspiracy has you in its grip.

You may soon be spending your way deep into debt, or at least wind up with a houseful of goods that don't actually give you much lasting pleasure — while you no longer have the money to do what you "really want" to do in life.

Problems created by the PIG-and-APE conspiracies take a tremendous toll. There are therapies and support groups for procrastinators and compulsive shoppers. Some people's lives are ruined by these unhealthy patterns and many more lives are diminished by them. They are the kinds of thought-and-behavior patterns that many of us get into routinely and *unknowingly*, barely realizing what we've done, or realizing it too late and feeling unable to correct it.

What's Driving You? — Some Simple Questions to Ask

Awareness is the key to heading off such predicaments, and sometimes the hardest part of building awareness is getting started. Knowing about the PIG, APE and Ego provides a simple set of guides to make it, well, simpler. But you don't have to confine yourself to learning these terms and using this framework.

It helps to have questions you can ask yourself in common everyday language — questions that will help you build your own, personalized "system" for becoming aware of what's driving you and making the distinctions you need to make. Here are several, starting with the most flat-out obvious.

> ➤ What is the fuel behind this act I am contemplating; what's driving me to it?

> ➤ What part of me "wins" if I do it?

> ➤ How long will the win last?

> ➤ Will it take me where I really want to go?

> ➤ Is it healthy or unhealthy?

And last but not least,

> ➤ Does anyone else win? Or just me, and maybe other people lose?

If the answer to any one of these questions feels shaky, you're after shaky gratification. It probably won't fulfill you and it's not likely to bear you along a magic-carpet ride of happiness and success. Even if the act looks good on paper, the motivation behind it — what's driving it — is highly suspect.

The questions contain some fairly broad words that you'll have to define for yourself, to a large extent: "healthy," "unhealthy," "win," "really want." That is as it should be. Becoming clearer on what's "healthy" for you, or what a "win" consists of, is part of the process of building awareness.

If the issue in question involves *not* doing something, just insert the word "not." What's driving me not to do it? What part of me wins if I don't do it?, and so on.

And speaking of words ...

About Words and Chatter

Words are the thinking mind's currency. The mind and all the creatures within it do their business in words. *You can hear them.*

We have chatter inside our heads continually. One person I know calls this chatter "squirrels on the roof." Another, in a pun on "verbalizing," calls it "gerbilizing."

Except for the times when you are engaged in very practical and logical types of problem-solving — like trying to figure out what you need to do before going away for the weekend, in which case you may actually write the words down on a list — the chatter is usually the mind and the Ego talking to each other. And that is a warning sign that they're up to something. They are not decoupled; they are in collusion to drive you in a direction that will waste your time or wind up being otherwise "unhealthy."

Can we turn off the chatter, as if turning off a radio? For brief periods at least, as in meditation: definitely. Many people have done this. But to shut off the mental flow of words permanently: no, I don't think so, nor would we want to. Despite their limitations, words themselves are much too useful to be done away with.

Words are *not* the real things that they refer to; they are only approximations of reality — "gravity," "Ego," "I think I'm falling in love," etc. Yet they are marvelous inventions, good enough for much of what we want to do with them. What we need to remember about words are the following points, which may be obvious but are still worth stating.

Words are attractive and seductive and not always helpful. For each of us, it's a toss-up as to which is more frequent: how often we fall for lies and nonsense, or how often we speak them. A lot of the chatter inside our heads is lies and nonsense, too, but it's compelling. The mind and the Ego are parts of you, and they know what can suck in the rest of you, so they say it.

There are flows of words in our heads that fall into gray areas, too; they might be mind-Ego chatter or they might be something more positive. When you sing a song in your head — or compose a song, or write a novel — that might be an inspired act in which the big YOU is accessing the larger intelligence, and passing what it finds there down to the mind to be put into words and symbols. Or, maybe not. Plenty of songs, books and other so-called creative works are Ego-driven, and it shows. For the words in our own heads, we may have to learn to make the distinction that code-breakers make: what part of the chatter is useful stuff — i.e., "intelligence" — and what part is noise.

Once we're able to hear the distinction, we can then learn to move past the Ego noise. Trying to make it stop won't work. That is an attempt to assert control, and controlling is the Ego's game: we can't use the Ego to shut off the Ego! Awareness operates more gently. We just recognize the chatter for what it is, then set it aside.

It's as if you were in a house while someone else is watching TV, and you would prefer not to be distracted, so you go to another room or step outside. In much the same way, we can learn to access a mental "space" of silence or stillness where the mind-chatter may still be audible, but it's like an inconsequential background noise. We aren't sucked into it.

With practice, we reach a stage at which we can set aside the mind-chatter *as needed*. We would set it aside in order to be at the level of full and direct awareness, beyond words. At that level, one might say that we move from words to music. We are able to think and act *harmoniously*. We can sense the flow that we need to go with, and go with it. At those moments we are completely happy in the moment, aware but untroubled, on the path to lasting fulfillment.

But of course one cannot just float suspended in that state like a solitary swimmer in the bliss-pool. We have to engage with life and with other people. We have to — gasp — *make choices*. And ideally, out of our growing awareness, we learn to make healthier choices. That's what the next chapter is about.

Chapter 7
MAKING CHOICES

We know that our lives are shaped by the choices we make. And when we think about life-shaping choices, we tend to think of the big ones: choosing a college, a career or a job; choosing a mate; choosing whether and when to have children, or where to live. These are certainly important decisions, not to be made lightly.

But our lives are also greatly affected by the little choices we make in the course of each day, by how we choose to handle each situation that comes up. It is my firm belief that the world constantly presents circumstances to help us evolve and grow. Thus we shape our lives by how we choose to think, feel, act, and live, from one moment to the next.

A little reflection will show that this is true in multiple ways. For one thing, the little choices we make now may determine the range of big choices that will be available to us later. When you're young, there are many times each day when you can choose to study and do your work or not. When it comes time to choose a college or job, you may have a handful of great offers to pick from, or slim pickings.

Likewise, each day in your dealings with other people you can choose to be honest or tricky, friendly or hostile, reliable or not. This will influence your reputation, your chances for success — and it will surely influence what sorts of people are willing to get close to you. When it comes to choosing a life partner, you'll probably get one you deserve.

The effects can also be more subtle, though equally profound. Throughout life, there are occasions when we can choose either to pursue status — to do something that we think will win the approval of others, and inflate our Egos by raising our standing in some hierarchy — or to do what we really feel inspired to do. For many of us these choices start in the early teens: do I try to hang out with the cool kids, the ones who look a certain way and know the certain stuff that seems to be oh, so important ... or should I just make friends with the kids who seem congenial to me?

And so it goes through the rest of life, in every matter from choosing our clothes to choosing how we spend our time. The choices aren't always clear-cut. Sometimes I attend a social event I don't "feel like" going to, mainly because it would be rude to stay away. But over time a *pattern of choices* will emerge in which we're either tending to pursue status and approval, or following some other call, a call that perhaps comes from somewhere larger. All of the choices may add up to make us into people who have deep and lasting happiness, or people with a persistent hollow feeling inside — a hollowness that the creatures within us will keep scrabbling in vain to fill.

So in countless ways, the little choices count, as well as the big ones. Over time, we develop patterns of choice-making, and they all come together to weave the fabric of our lives. They can determine whether we'll be happy and productive even in the face of adversity ... or miserable in the midst of plenty.

In this chapter we'll talk about the big choices, but maybe more about the small ones. There are so many of them, so many opportunities to learn and practice every day, that it literally may be more "practical" if we dwell mostly on these.

In the last part of the book we'll use the notion of "Life Spaces" to categorize common choice-making situations — choices you make in regard to Your Self, your relations with Your Life Partner, Your Friends, Your Work, Your Money, and Your Children. I'll then present stories to illustrate some typical types of choices you might face in each Life Space. The purpose of the stories is to expand awareness of how people's choices work, or fail to work, in particular areas of everyday life.

While the stories are like "case studies," this chapter is more like Choice-Making 101. Here, we're going to take a wide-ranging view and look at a few general principles or approaches that might apply in many situations. In the process, we'll also point out some classic traps to avoid. Let's start with a favorite of mine.

The Art of Living Two Days at a Time

A core principle for making choices of any kind is simply this: we want to make them from *our highest level of awareness*. To put in language that some people might use, we want to become "enlightened" so we can make enlightened choices. And one of the first pitfalls we might come across is a tricky one, because it lies right in the path to awareness and enlightenment.

We are often told that to be truly aware and enlightened, we must become fully present in the present moment, living in the Now. One of my favorite books, mentioned in Chapter 5, is called *The Power of Now*. The twelve-step community, which has helped millions of people, has a slogan we're all familiar with: to live "One Day at a Time."

Therein lies the pitfall. Listening to these maxims, we can be tempted to think they mean living as if there is no tomorrow. *Hey, I'm an enlightened being. I know that right now is all there is, so I just do what my inner voice tells me to do right now, today, and it's all going to work out.*

In a PIG's eye it will. When you live every day as if there's no tomorrow, the main question is, how many years will it take before you realize that it might've been a good idea to plan ahead a little? Yet on the other hand, you don't want to miss the fullness of each moment and each day by merely living them as a means to some future end, which may never arrive. Who knows what is going to change next week or five years from now? Will you still be around then; do you have a guaranteed contract? I know too many people who unknowingly plan and execute "Life 1" up to age 60 or so, in order to enjoy "Life 2" after retirement, thereby missing a lot of the joy of the prime years of adulthood.

There has to be a balance between the two extremes of living only for today and living only for the future, and it's not very difficult to find. I believe a good balance would be:

Live Two Days at a Time.

In other words: by all means, yes, "Be Here Now" and *attend fully to the issues and the people before you today*. But at the same time, be always aware *not to do anything that could jeopardize your tomorrow*. At the end of each day you might ask: What did I learn today? What can I do different tomorrow? Then "just live it" the next day. Today and tomorrow, today and tomorrow. *Life is a repeating series of todays and tomorrows.*

Any of us can take it in those chunks. It's like driving with an awareness of where you are, but also of the road up ahead, which we all do when we're driving intelligently. Maybe once in a while we pull off to the side to study a map or ask directions. That's like occasionally stepping out of the routines in life to assess things and to plan long-term, which is also an excellent idea. But most of the time it's where you are, plus the road ahead. And so in life: today and tomorrow, two days at a time.

Don't Get Caught in the Rapids

Even living two days at a time can be tough, however, in our modern culture. We live in a society focused on rapid if not instant results — one where consumers use instant credit to buy plug-and-play products. One where if you're not an overnight hit, the solution is an instant makeover.

One where the sublime joy of living in the moment somehow gets confused with the notion that we ought to be able to do anything and everything, all the time, in every moment. Like sharing every thought as it arises, with everybody we know, and getting so caught up in texting that we're never really present — never really where we are — in any moment.

This is very strange. Not too long ago, people were suspicious of the word "instant." It usually meant something inferior, like instant coffee, not as good as the brewed kind. Also not too long ago, it was common to laugh at the people who constantly felt driven to have the newest and latest versions of stuff: the latest fashions, the new Buick. That was called keeping up with the Joneses and it was seen for what it is — a vain attempt to appear smart and original, whereas in fact there may be nothing more stale and imitative than to be always chasing the newest thing.

Today the perception has changed. The general rule is *the faster the better* and the word that's viewed with universal suspicion is ... "slow." You don't even want be slow to answer a question. In the time it takes you to reflect, people will think you are either clueless or trying to hide something, or they'll be impatient with the silence. Try this experiment: when you are with some people, start talking, then pause in the middle of a sentence or at the end. See if the group waits calmly for you to proceed. Typically there will be signs of discomfort very quickly, then someone will jump in to break the awkwardness. Few people still believe the old adage that "silence is golden." Silence is considered bad — it's what radio broadcasters call "dead air," and you can't have dead air.

Today it is not seen as vanity, but as a duty, to arm yourself and your kids with the latest goods, services and information for every purpose. The philosophy is like Darwinism on speed: creatures that are slow to adapt lose an edge and die, so don't be one. And if you pass up a chance for instant cash, instant rewards or instant pain relief, you're just being foolish. You are missing a chance to take advantage of what's out there waiting for you. Why so slow?

We now live in a choice-making environment that might be called double-fast. The choices promise fast payback, and they have to be made fast. Letting ourselves get caught in that pattern doesn't seem like the healthiest way to live.

The key to a rewarding life is to make choices aimed at building profound happiness — the kind that stems from an essential joy in life, the kind that is likely to last — as distinct from chasing opportunities to feel good or avoid pain right away.

And what's wrong with feeling good? Nothing, as long as it doesn't undermine our chances for profound and lasting happiness. But too often we make feel-good, pain-avoiding choices that do exactly that.

To give an obvious example, right now I could spend the next hour on the Internet, reading fascinating news and gossip. That would be fun. However I wouldn't finish writing this part of the book, and I believe that writing it and being able to share it with others will be much more deeply rewarding.

Yet the lure of electronic media is very hard to resist. The constant barrage of news flashes and personal messages can make it seem as if each item is urgent: *If it's there, it must be worthwhile.*

Otherwise it wouldn't be there, would it? There is growing evidence that this barrage has negative effects. To quote an article on the subject, from the *New York Times*:

> Scientists say juggling e-mail, phone calls and other incoming information can change how people think and behave. They say our ability to focus is being undermined by bursts of information.
>
> These play to a primitive impulse to respond to immediate opportunities and threats. The stimulation provokes excitement — a dopamine squirt — that researchers say can be addictive. In its absence, people feel bored.

Is there a phrase that looks familiar here? Yes, it's the "primitive impulse to respond to immediate opportunities and threats." In other words, the PIG and the APE. Ironically, in a hard-working country built upon the old ethic of delayed gratification, we've created an environment that conditions us to make PIG and APE choices.

Along with undermining our ability to "focus," these choices also hamper our ability to find joy in the moment and to build long-term happiness. Nor is this type of choice-making confined to the virtual world of the Internet. Other, more insidious examples abound in so-called real life:

➤ To have some peace and quiet at home, I can give in to my child if she throws a tantrum.

> ➤ Or to enjoy a romantic evening with my wife, I can try dodging and joking my way around the difficult "issues" that she's been wanting to discuss.

Each of these choices might make things easier, for today. But in each case I'd be short-circuiting the process of building healthy relationships with the people in my family — while setting precedents that are bound to lead to trouble down the road.

And the list of sub-optimal choices goes on:

> ➤ To buy something I want, right away, I can borrow the money.

> ➤ To get more work done faster, I can cut corners. The customers probably won't notice, and if they complain, we'll fix it then.

> ➤ To build up my Ego, I can poke fun at other people or tear them down.

> ➤ To relieve stress, I can eat and drink as much as I want. And then put on my running shorts to try to run off the calories, or try that diet that promises a ten-pound weight loss in two weeks.

All across the land, millions of us are making such choices every day. That's why so many of us are in debt and overweight. That's why insults and sound bites prevail over decency and deliberation in public affairs, and so on. We live in a society often dominated by PIGs and APEs running untamed in the service of gigantic Egos.

And please don't think that I am merely off on a tirade about "what's wrong with America." You will find things to be much the same in other countries. Maybe worse.

So what are we to do? Just recognize that in order to make a difference in our own lives, and perhaps in society at large, we need to go against the grain. And not by being a noisy rebel but by looking inward. The grain we need to go against just might be the grain of our own PIG, APE and Ego. *It all starts with you*, with your ability to live as the big YOU.

The Third Choice — and a Third Level of Choosing

Three is often seen as a magical number, as in "The third time is the charm." And so it is with making choices. You may have noticed that when you're mulling a decision and looking at options, very often it's the third choice — the third option that comes to mind — which turns out to be the best.

There's not much mystery to that. Many times when you sit down to make a choice, either alone or with others, you are faced with a yes-or-no, this-or-that type of decision. *Should we eat out or stay in? Do I mow the lawn or watch the ball game?* Even in cases with a lot of options, you'll typically try to narrow down the choices by making a series of yes-no decisions. If you're deciding where to apply to college, what about Penn State? You will either put that school on your list or cross it off. Then you'll do the same yes-no process with Rutgers, Virginia Tech and a bunch of others, until you have a workable list of schools to which you'll actually make visits and send applications.

Here's a trap, however. In any yes-no, this-or-that situation, it is possible to get locked into thinking that the two options in front of you are the *only* ones. As you may recall from Chapter 3, earlier in my life I thought the only two life options were to be a Cricket or an Ant. Or to alternate between the two, as in being a hard-working Ant most of the time but taking Cricket breaks to dissipate myself in fleeting pleasures.

Sometimes there are in fact only two options: you can get on the bus before it pulls away, or not. But sometimes there is a third which may be a synthesis of the two, or a shifting of your frame of reference to see a higher-level option that's *beyond* the two you thought you were stuck with. This is what happened for me when I discovered a way of living beyond the Cricket and the Ant.

And since the third option usually comes from a larger intelligence, a larger or more sophisticated point of view, it's not surprising that it often turns out to be the "best." That was my case as I experienced a higher level of being and awareness.

Now let's investigate that further. If there is a higher level of being and awareness, might it not also be a higher level of choosing — a higher state from which to make choices? And if so, wouldn't it be a good idea to talk about elevating to that third level, so that if needed we can make as many choices as possible from that level?

Of course it would. There are essentially three levels of choosing:

> ➤ Level 1 choices are made by the PIG and APE. You are not really "in control" at all.

> ➤ Level 2 choices are made by engaging the mind. Here, you think over the choice logically, and also add time into the equation — that is, take a longer view of the consequences. Typically you think you are in control ... although often, it is your Ego that's in charge.

> ➤ Level 3 choices are made by accessing a higher level of intelligence, beyond the Egoic mind. Your choices can have far-reaching impact but the notion of "control" no longer applies, because you have transcended control. You don't need it. You are acting *in harmony* with the world and with life.

These levels of choosing are worth examining in some detail. They correspond to the three levels of awareness we learned about in Chapter 5, so there will be some things here that are a recap, but also a number of angles we haven't looked at.

Level 1 Choices:
The 'Immediate and Certain' vs. 'Future and Uncertain' Trap

As noted above, at Level 1 you let your PIG and APE make your choices for you. At this level you will probably eat out most of the time, and the lawn might not be mowed until you pay someone to do it.

Choices that are truly unhealthy also are made at this level, such as the choice to smoke cigarettes. Why do people smoke, despite the evidence against it? Why do so many still find it so hard to quit? One answer, pointed out by Aubrey Daniels in his book *Bringing Out the Best in People*, may simply be as follows.

The rewards are *Immediate and Certain,* while the major negative consequences are *Future and Uncertain.*

The "rewards" that people get from tobacco, such as stress relief and mild intoxication, happen right away and they're practically guaranteed. The big negatives that are so often emphasized, such as lung cancer and emphysema, probably won't come until many years after today's cigarettes and they may not come at all.

The PIG likes Immediate and Certain rewards. The APE doesn't worry about Future and Uncertain negatives.

Conversely, this may also explain why you don't get around to writing the great novel you've planned. The negatives, like the time and effort you will have to put in, are Immediate and Certain, which means the APE will avoid them. The rewards lie in the Future and are Uncertain, so the PIG isn't interested.

The moral of the story is that on the choice-making level of the PIG and the APE, *"Immediate and Certain" will beat "Future and Uncertain" every time.*

Some people find a way out of this trap by using mental tricks that tip the balance of the equation, as it were. For instance, they manage to stop smoking not by reminding themselves of the diseases they might get many years down the road, but rather by focusing on the negatives which are every bit as Immediate and Certain as the rewards are. If you smoke, here are some negatives guaranteed to show up right away:

> You'll spend money on cigarettes.

> Your breath and your clothes will smell bad.

> Other people will notice and disapprove.

> In most public places, you will have to leave every time you want to light up.

> You'll be short winded, and so on.

For *some* people, adding up these Immediate and Certain negatives — and deciding that they outweigh the Immediate and Certain rewards — is enough to help them quit.

I used to think that "tilting the equation" in this way was the solution to most of life's choice-making traps. I figured you could also use the method to get rolling on a project you've been putting off, like that novel. Just surround yourself with positive reinforcements that are as Immediate and Certain as the time and effort required. If you start the novel, you can join a writers' group, and that will be interesting. If you write a chapter every week, you can show the chapters to friends who will enjoy them. You'll have the satisfaction of being able to say that you *are* a writer, as opposed to somebody who's merely thinking about it. Just keep adding Immediate and Certain reinforcements, and you'll be on your way!

That's what I used to think. Now I take a more measured view. This form of self-manipulation can work for some people, in some cases, just as it does with smoking. If it works for one of your tough challenges, you are welcome to it. But there are also limitations to this approach. What it really is, is an escalation to Level 2 choice-making.

Level 2 Choices:
Engaging the Mind and Adding Time

On the second level we use reason and logic to "manage" the PIG and APE, and also to analyze the situation. The rewards we get, as in the novel-writing example, may feel emotional but we're using reason and logic to make the choices that bring them about. At this level we are also apt to take a longer-term view. We look forward to the rewards accruing gradually as we stay away from cigarettes or keep working on the novel, so in that sense we're "adding time" into the choice.

Most of us try to operate at Level 2 when confronted with big choices, such as about college. *Would Penn State be a good fit for me? Well, let's see. Let's make a list of the pros and cons.* Studying all the factors and weighing them up seems to be a scientific approach, so we assume it's how smart people make their decisions, and it's what we do when we feel the need to make a really smart choice. Level 2 is also where we operate when we make "responsible" choices like getting after that lawn. *The grass needs to be mowed. I agreed that it's my chore, and I won't have time later. Therefore, I mow.*

There's a lot to be said for Level 2. With any big choice, especially if the situation is complicated, it pays to give it due diligence. You don't want to miss anything important. You also don't want to get sucked into an impulse choice, like buying the wrong car for the wrong reason, and a systematic approach can help avoid that pitfall too. As part of the process it's common to spell out *the criteria by which you're going to make your choice.* We'll do this when looking for a home to buy or rent: It can't cost more than so much, and the lower the better. Maximum 30-minute commute to work, and the shorter the better, et cetera.

Finally, Level 2 helps you take a rigorous look at the long-term consequences. When they're tempted to pick up a drink, some recovering alcoholics use a technique called "Think the drink through." *If I have just one, will I want another? Yeah, probably. And what comes next, and then what, and where will that lead?*

For all these reasons Level 2 tends to be viewed as the highest and best level of choice-making. But there is much evidence to the contrary.

Where Level 2 Choices Fall Short

The first pitfall is that our minds can play tricks on us. In some traditions, it's referred to as the "monkey mind." The most logical mind is fully capable of believing anything it wants to believe. History is filled with the stories of wealthy, successful people who lost their fortunes by falling for investment schemes that were too good to be true — it happens on Wall Street all the time — and some great scientists have wasted their later years by thinking they could find the ultimate answer to the riddles of the universe: they get obsessed with trying to prove a grand "theory of everything" which almost anyone can tell is bogus.

We saw in the last chapter what drives these kinds of mistakes. Our thinking minds can get hijacked by our inner creatures. We then use the mind to rationalize emotional decisions that are really made by the PIG or the APE, or to pursue unrealistic Ego goals.

And even when the mind isn't playing tricks, it can miss the mark. We've all had times when we went through a perfectly logical thinking process ... looked at what our calculations and cogitations told us to do ... and yet said, "No, no, that can't be it." Everything says house X is the right one to buy. It's got a nice price, the rooms you need, a high-ranked school district for the kids ... but it just doesn't feel like home.

I remember a big business deal at a firm where I worked. We studied the deal carefully in advance. All the checkboxes were checked and all the numbers added up. The only red flag was a hard-to-define hunch on my part that something didn't feel right. I couldn't put a rational finger on it, so we went ahead. Then, after the deal was done, we learned what the something was. If you had a dollar for every business decision that is made this way, only to turn out this way, you'd have a nice business.

So what's the solution? Throw logic to the wind and go with your gut? Some people do that, and some pay the price. "I know he keeps losing his jobs, and sometimes he cheats on me, and yes he has a little bit of a criminal record. But I'm going to marry him."

Other people go in the opposite direction. They try to expand their logical decision-making systems to account for the so-called intangibles. Maybe in comparing houses, you could set up a point system and say that "feels like home" is worth 50 points.

In fact there are computer programs for making every kind of choice imaginable, from picking stocks to picking a potential mate to date, and they use scoring systems very similar to this. The basic idea is to take all of the factors that can influence a choice, including those we don't usually "measure" — such as value judgments and feelings, or unknowns and what-ifs — and assign numbers to them. That way, so the thinking goes, everything can be reckoned together and better judgments will result.

Some of these computer programs work extremely well. Chess-playing programs can beat human world champions, for instance. Using the type of system I've just described, they relentlessly calculate which move — out of the many possible moves on a chessboard, at a given time — is likely to be "worth" the most towards winning the game.

You could say that decision programs, in chess and other fields, represent the ultimate in Level 2 choice-making. But now let's look at the limitations. To begin with, chess may be complicated but it's a controlled game, totally rule-bound. A knight or a queen on a chessboard can only move in certain prescribed ways, whereas that may not be true of the knight in shining armor in your life, or the drama queen in your life. They are liable to play by rules of their own. You won't find a computer program that can deal with their moves.

And as I noted in Chapter 5, if you do have a tricky relationship in your life, trying to "reason with" the person usually doesn't work so well either. All of this points to a limitation of Level 2 choice-making in general. Logical approaches break down in cases where the "rules" and patterns, or the people, are just too irrational or illogical in their own right. In a revealing book called *Predictably Irrational,* the behavioral economist Dan Ariely showed how people can be irrational even when they think they're thinking rationally. So if you want to deal with these cases in a systematic way, you need a higher-level system.

Now here's another limitation of Level 2. Although we have many life situations which can, in fact, be handled by applying logical rules, the rules are *different* from one type of situation to the next. That's why the chess-playing program can't help you do your math homework, and the program that chooses the fastest route for driving to Jerry's house can't tell you how to invest your money. Different kinds of choice-making rules apply in each case and different kinds of information are needed, too. Nobody yet has been able to write a single computer program that can handle it all.

Long before the invention of computers, people also noticed that all of the rules and information you need for making all sorts of choices can't be carried around in one person's head. That's why they invented maps, and cookbooks, and reference books and instruction manuals of every kind. You could just look up what you needed. And if you were caught someplace where you had to make a choice and you didn't have your library with you? Too bad.

Today, of course, some people figure they have found a way around this problem. It is to carry a handy portable device, like a smartphone, that's loaded with all sorts of choice-making programs and has Internet access too. Now you're ready. Whenever you're faced with a decision, just pull the little thing out of your pocket and there you go.

But here again, limitations crop up. For instance: *The kid's throwing a temper tantrum? Okay, wait a minute while I look up what to do. I SAID, WAIT A MINUTE while I ...* How fast can you scroll?

And always, there is the limitation we mentioned earlier. A lot of the time, logical Level 2 choice-making, whether it's done by a computer or done in your head, will give you an answer that simply doesn't seem right. *Is this really the fastest way to Jerry's?*

Maybe the mapping program doesn't "know" the roads in your area the way that you do. Maybe you, yourself, get stuck in traffic or take ill-advised shortcuts that turn into long-cuts when you are picking directions on your own, and you are in such a hurry that you aren't accessing that higher level of knowing.

The bottom line is: Level 2 choice-making can only take us so far. It is done from the "Semi-Aware" level of awareness that we discussed in Chapter 5.

Logic, reason, and computer intelligence have their uses, to be sure. But beyond a certain point, we need to go — beyond. We may need to build on what our Level 2 processes have told us and take an extra step ... or in other cases, transcend what they've told us and choose on a higher basis. Either way, we move to Level 3.

Level 3 Choices:
Beyond Logic and the Thinking Mind

Much of what's worth saying about this level of choosing can be summed up in one sentence. Level 3 choices come from Awareness.

To help make this clear, let's make a distinction. There are two words that often get used as if they mean the same thing: "logic" and "sense." As if a phrase like "Use your common sense!" means the same as "Be logical!" Actually they are very different. Logic is what the thinking mind does. It's not the same as *opening up your senses* — using the "common senses" that we all have — to be fully aware of what is inside you and around you. The first is Level 2, the other can be Level 3.

Logic, as any philosopher will tell you, *starts from assumptions* and then works from them, step by step, to reach a conclusion or a choice. It works great ... as long as the assumptions are solid. But if they aren't, logic can take you miles off the track.

Maybe your PIG and Ego are telling you that you absolutely have to have a new wardrobe, a better boyfriend or whatever, and then all your problems will be solved. So your thinking mind starts from that assumption, making the logical choices and taking the logical steps that get you to the goal ...and whoa, it's all wrong! You're still not happy! Entire books have been written about the many different ways in which flawed assumptions, plus perfectly logical execution, add up to disaster.

Sense, on the other hand, is all about the awareness that comes from literally sensing what is so. It asks questions like *What's going on here? How do I fit into this? What am I up to, anyway?* ... and then proceeds from what it learns. The intent of sense is to get to the heart of things; to detect — and therefore show us how to affect — the flow of things.

Let's go back to the kid throwing the temper tantrum. A tantrum is often described as "a fit with a purpose." In other words, the person is doing it to get something he or she wants. If you operate on Level 2, you'll probably start from the assumption that that's what is going on when your child explodes. This leads to logical thinking about things like how to teach him that he can't always have what he wants.

But wait. What if this isn't just a fit with a *greedy* purpose? What if there is something deeper behind it, something the child is genuinely upset about, or afraid of? Might he be terrified that unless he is allowed to do such-and-such, the boogieman will get him, or he'll be a bad person? And if that should be the case, then you have to ask: is the child's concern a legitimate one? Or is his own budding Ego, perhaps, creating this fear?

If you operate from full and calm awareness, you may be led to a Level 3 choice quite different from the one you would have made at Level 2. Not only does this awareness allow you to sense what is going on with others, it enables you to sense what's going on inside yourself so that you don't react rashly, and it can open you up to creative solutions. Here is a true story to illustrate what I mean.

Some years ago a colleague of mine, we'll call him Steve, got unpleasant news from the police. His teenaged son had been caught shoplifting. Although shoplifting may not seem to be the most heinous of crimes, learning that one's child has committed any kind of crime can be a severe blow to a parent. In particular, it can be a blow to the parent's Ego. It's as if the incident tells the world that you are a bad parent; that you haven't been able to control your child; that you've been teaching the wrong values and so forth.

And a lot of parents react from their Egos. Sometimes, the first thing they'll say when they are face-to-face with the kid is to shout, "How could you do this to me?" This is then followed by more yelling, and by punishments meted out in a spirit that is truly punishing.

Steve's response was different. No yelling or recriminations. Like most parents, he chose to punish his child after the authorities had released him, but Steve's choice was a creative one made in the spirit of *correcting* his son. Steve gave the boy a homework assignment which amounted to a huge punishment for a teenager who liked to play and disliked writing. For several weeks, he was to spend two hours per day at the library, doing research on shoplifting and its effects. At the end he was to write a paper on the subject.

In the course of this exercise, Steve's son learned a great deal. He learned that shoplifting isn't the victimless crime some people think it is when they steal from chain stores owned by big corporations, as he had done. He learned how the costs and consequences get passed along to all of us, how businesses have to change the way they operate to try to deal with shoplifting, and how the shoplifters themselves are negatively affected.

These lessons, combined with Steve's clear-headed handling of the whole situation, were extremely effective. The son never got into trouble with the law again and went on to become a happy, responsible adult. That's the power of Level 3. Moreover, the story leads us to another vital element of choices at this level.

Never from the Ego

Level 3 choices are never made with the intention of serving the Ego.

The word "intention" is key, because some cases arise in which Level 3 choices provide an "Ego boost" as a sort of side effect. The classic example is an act of generosity or benevolence. Operating in the light of full awareness, we choose to do something that really helps somebody else. It's an inspired choice, beyond what anyone would expect, and we pass up a chance for our own gain or pleasure in order to do it. Yet not too surprisingly, the result may feed our Ego just a little bit. It may feed the part of our mind-made identity that thinks "I am a saintly person, always looking out for others before myself."

While it's natural to feel satisfaction at what we've done, we have to be watchful. Are we feeling the joy of being and giving, or is it Ego satisfaction? This is one reason why some people only give to charity anonymously, and some even try to keep a low profile when doing personal favors. They don't want to be drawn down the path of feeding the Ego. They know that the path leads to unhealthy states of being — such as feeling resentment if we think our efforts aren't properly appreciated or recognized.

My son noticed this danger when he was just ten. He had pitched in to help us do a big favor for another family. That family sent us a thank-you note, thanking my wife and me but forgetting to name my son. He stared at the note and said, "I'm offended." Then he corrected himself by saying, "No, my Ego is offended." Wish we all could be so aware!

And the greater danger, of course, is that Ego gratification will become part of our motive for doing benevolent acts in the first place. This can cause all kinds of mischief. For instance, if we shower attention on people expecting them to feel obligated to us, *they* will resent it. Or, they'll feel guilty about not showing proper gratitude in return. Some parents are skilled at making their children feel guilty this way.

Furthermore, if we're looking for Ego rewards when we give our time, money or effort, it will influence our choice of whom we give to, and for what. Instead of helping people who could genuinely use the help, maybe we'll help those who are most likely to show gratitude. Instead of "doing the right thing" — i.e., what needs to be done — we do what will bring us glory or protect our standing.

These patterns are ancient and one can see them everywhere. Shakespeare summed them up in his play *King Lear,* about the old king who brings his whole kingdom to grief by leaving it to the wicked daughters who are willing to flatter his Ego, while shutting out the honest daughter who won't. In modern-day politics, we're shocked when politicians betray their principles by failing to stand up for worthy causes or for needy groups of citizens ... while going out on a limb to help the people who can deliver the votes to keep them in office.

It is easy for any of us to slide into making choices of this type in our daily lives. We can avoid them by being keenly aware of our motivations, especially Ego motivations.

As the Bob Dylan song says, "You're gonna have to serve somebody." You can serve your Ego, or you can make Level 3 choices that serve the world, but you can't do both. The choice is yours.

Intuition, not Instinct

One final distinction is also useful to discern, as we develop the art of making choices from Level 3. Again, it's a distinction between two things that frequently get confused as being the same: "instinct" and "intuition."

It can be hard to tell the difference, because while instinct and intuition are not at all the same, they tend to feel the same. They may both show up as a sort of gut feeling, or a sudden voice telling us that *this* is what we ought to do. And we jumble the two in our language as well. When certain people seem to have a knack for getting flashes of insight that lead to brilliant choices, we may say they have "great instincts," when in fact we mean they're very good at being open to intuition. It helps immensely to make the distinction, because this is more than a matter of being picky about words.

Instinct comes from our animal nature, from the PIG and the APE. It is useful on the raw, primitive level of survival, as when our instincts do things like making us jump out of the way of actual, physical threats. However on the more sophisticated levels of human interaction and choosing, instinct can be unreliable or downright misleading — as when our instincts make us "jump to conclusions" or "jump all over somebody" who is trying to be helpful.

We sometimes talk about "blind instinct" and in fact, that's an apt term, because instinct *is* blind. When we allow instinct alone to drive us, it's like flying blind. We just go racing in the direction that the animal engine pulls us, often into trouble.

Intuition comes from awareness, and it comes through the natural self. It allows us to make connections that perhaps we can't put into words, but yet are clear and shining once made. It's not blindness. It's vision.

Here are a couple of ways to tell the difference, when that gut feeling or that sudden voice comes upon us:

> ➤ Instinct feels urgent, even frenzied. There's a tremendous compulsion to act on what it's telling us — almost like a commander shouting an urgent order. Intuition may bring a rush of sensation, but it's more like a flood of delight or astonishment — followed by certainty that *we* will know what to do.

> ➤ Instinct is a reaction, usually a predictable reaction. It will often drive us to do the same darned thing we've done countless times before in situations like this one. Intuition leads us to a response, often a creative response.

Instincts may feel familiar when they strike, because you've always had them. Intuition is a key element of Level 3 choices and you can *learn* to be open to it. That is, you can learn to have greater and keener intuition, and have it visit you regularly instead of showing up as an occasional surprise visitor. And there's no bag of tricks to learn. All it takes is being aware.

Awareness-Based Learning

So it goes, too, with just about any aspect of learning to make healthier, happier choices. In this chapter I've suggested some useful concepts and general principles. Some more of them will be illustrated in the next chapter. But mainly, we learn to make choices by being aware.

Full awareness is an inside-outside deal: aware of what's going on inside us, and around us. The two go together naturally, so naturally that as we become fully aware, we may actually notice less of a boundary between our "selves" and the "outside world." Those two blend together as well.

In practical terms, the inner awareness shows us what's driving us and how we are operating as we go about making a choice, while the outer awareness lets in everything else. And "everything else" includes not only the environment but also the larger intelligence. That should cover what we need.

This type of learning, which I call awareness-based learning, has a long tradition in many cultures and is being used increasingly in Western society, even in areas like learning to play tennis and golf. Awareness-based learning is distinct from instructional or how-to learning, which consists mainly of learning specific procedures, tips and techniques. You can see that type in traditional tennis or golf lessons. They're full of pointers on how to grip the racquet or the club, and how your elbows, hips, and every other part of your body ought to be positioned or moving as you take a swing. The lessons of the awareness-based type, championed by Tim Gallwey and others, focus much more on being aware of the only thing that matters: hitting the ball. How the racquet face, or the club face, makes contact.

One problem with the instructional, how-to approach in these sports is that people's minds can get so tied up in following all the pointers that they tie themselves in knots. The students can get so self-conscious and awkward that their stroke is a mess, and then … yep, the answer is more lessons. When it comes to learning to make choices in life, there is an added problem, which we've already seen. Life is much larger and more complex than any game. It's impossible to master enough specific rules and pointers that would be needed for the many situations that come up.

So a key to awareness-based learning, in sports or in life, is to have as few guidelines as possible: just a basic set that equip you to "learn to learn" as you go along. The rest will come if you keep your eye on the ball — focus on that inner-outer awareness.

And by the way, awareness means awareness, period. Being aware of what's going on inside you, for instance, does not mean constantly judging or trying to control what's going on inside you. That's an Ego game, and it will also tie you up in self-*consciousness* — the self-criticism and self-correction on half a dozen fronts at once that messes up the poor golfers. Awareness alone will take you much farther.

I'll say more about awareness-based learning in Chapter 9, The State of Joy. That will include coming back to a topic we started addressing here, but didn't finish: changing unhealthy habits, such as smoking. Right now, let's expand on Level 3 choice-making in its highest form, as it relates to Expanding Creativity.

Chapter 8

EXPANDING CREATIVITY

Creativity is often defined as the act of bringing something "new and valuable" into the world. When people make a work of art or compose a beautiful song, they express themselves while bringing enjoyment to others, and creativity can be a very practical matter as well. Indeed, I am sitting here this morning wearing and using works of creativity.

I am looking through eyeglasses — an invention made nearly a thousand years ago, by someone now unknown — at the screen of a computer, the combined product of many different discoveries and inventions. And on the computer is a draft of this book, a creative work which I hope will be of practical value to you.

It's no wonder that creative ability itself is highly valued. Today there are entire industries devoted to helping you develop that ability. In your city right now, creativity consultants are waiting for you to call and order a training program for your business or nonprofit group. At a university near you, psychologists are in the process of creating experiments to study the creative process. And if you were to read just a fraction of the books that have already been written about creativity, you'd never have time to practice it.

Why then should you read this chapter, when I am not a certified creativity expert? Because what we've been learning about the PIG, the APE and the Ego applies to creativity. By moving beyond these creatures, and expanding our awareness, we expand our ability to create.

People sometimes speak of creativity as a special "gift" that some of us are blessed with, to a degree that most of us can never achieve. But even the experts agree that that's not true. The renowned psychologist Margaret Boden called it a "romantic myth."

The greatest gift is awareness. It's there for each of us. If we exercise this gift daily we can learn to be more creative in more ways — not only in artistic work or invention, but in our personal lives and relationships.

In the next few pages we'll look at some examples of creativity in everyday life. They show how accessible the gift really is, and they illustrate some principles that apply to *any* kind of creative activity. The first one is a true story, told to me by a person close to the situation.

In a pleasant small town in the South, there lived an elderly gentleman who had become a recluse. He was a retired engineer who had bought a pretty little house and settled into it with his wife. They had not been the most public couple to begin with. Then his wife passed away and, as they say, he went into a shell.

There were occasional sightings — somebody would spot him in the supermarket, or taking a walk alone — but other than those rare times, it seemed that he never left the house. And the house had turned into a specimen of utter neglect. Parts were literally falling off. The yard was a mess. One could only wonder how things were inside. A grim joke had it that the one sign of hope was the deteriorating roof. Surely it let in rainwater, so maybe the neighbors didn't have to worry so much about the place being a fire hazard.

People in the neighborhood were at a loss for what to do. They pitied the old fellow but they were starting to see him as a *problem*. Some tried dropping by to invite him to church, or to go bowling, anything to get him back in circulation because after all, it isn't healthy for a person to be alone. The invitations and platitudes didn't work any better than the threats to report him to the housing inspector or call in the lawyers.

Finally one neighbor found a way to break through. Strolling by the house one evening, he saw the old gentleman on the porch. The neighbor ignored the man's forbidding stare and, searching for something to say, said what a nice porch it was. The old man grudgingly admitted it would be all right except for the front door. That hardly seemed to be the house's major problem, but as the man pointed out, the door was an unfinished one that needed painting: "Took me a couple of years to get around to hanging it. Still haven't painted it." The neighbor managed to draw out a little more small talk, about such topics as what color the door ought to be, and that was the end of the encounter.

A couple of days later, the neighbor returned to the house with paint and tools. He didn't bother knocking. He just spread out a drop cloth, pried the lid off the paint and set to work. Then came the moment when the door handle clicked and the door opened. The old gentleman beheld the scene, so thunderstruck that he could only ask the obvious question: "What are you doing?"

The neighbor gave the obvious answer, and though it didn't break the entire ice field right away, of course it led to a longer conversation while he finished the job. Within weeks, more jobs were done. And the two men were spending hours sitting together, sipping tea and talking ...

I think you'll agree that what this good neighbor was inspired to do was something "new and valuable." Now let's see what the story can tell us about awareness and creativity.

Inside the Creative Act

In 1879, Thomas Edison created an invention that became the universal symbol for creativity: the light bulb. It has been pictured lighting up over people's heads in cartoons ever since. The trouble is, one can be tempted to think that's all it takes to be creative:

finding a way to make the light bulb go on, learning some tricks to conjure up brilliant ideas. But there is much more to it.

For one thing, having a brilliant idea isn't the end of the process. If the friendly neighbor in our story had merely had an idea — *wow, maybe I could paint the guy's door* — and hadn't done anything about it, we would have no story to tell. His idea could have died at birth just as millions of bright ideas die every day. For instance, his APE could have killed the idea by filling his head with a bunch of pain-avoiding and Ego-protecting chatter. *Come on, it's painful just standing here trying to talk to this old man. He thinks you're a pain in the butt anyway!* And so on, and so forth.

But evidently that didn't happen. Or if it did, the neighbor was able to recognize it for the mind-chatter that it was, and therefore couldn't be swayed by it.

Furthermore: if the Ego and its animal creatures are in control, they can prevent ideas of this type from occurring at all. So the fact that the good neighbor even had the idea — even was willing to stop and have the conversation that *led* to the idea — suggests that his Ego was not in control going into the encounter. Which brings up another important point.

Just as having a brilliant idea is not the end of the creative process, it's not the beginning of the process, either.

As Louis Pasteur said, "Chance favors the prepared mind." Pasteur was a scientist and he was referring mainly to the need to do one's homework. If you study your subject diligently, learning all about it that you can, then you will be prepared to notice the unexpected little things that often turn out to be the clues to major discoveries. That's good advice in any field. For instance, the more I learn about my children and what they are up to, the better prepared I will be to notice when they're up to something unusual!

But merely learning a lot of facts isn't enough. Another kind of preparation is vital. In order to notice what others might overlook — and in order to be open to brilliant ideas — we have to prepare by being aware. Ideally we are constantly and vigilantly aware, using our radar, because we never know where a clue may turn up or when an inspiration may occur. However we can't notice anything that our inner creatures prevent us from noticing. Thus, one essential way of having a "prepared mind" is to de-couple the mind from the Ego, and be at the highest level of awareness.

So it was in our story of the good neighbor. Only a person who was well prepared, by being in excellent *inner condition,* could have navigated that initial encounter with the old gentleman. None of it was planned; the whole thing just unfolded. Imagine yourself in the neighbor's place: you are strolling down the street and there the old guy is. Most people in the neighborhood have made one of two choices, either to deal with him as an object of pity, or as a nuisance and a danger. You are open to a third choice, which is to deal with him as a human being.

How obvious! Why of course; that's what he is! And yet, so much of creativity, like so much of what I have talked about throughout this book, just comes down to seeing what is.

Maybe your Ego could be threatened or angered by the old man's forbidding demeanor, but the big YOU isn't ... and when

YOU search for something to say for openers, is it just a lucky coincidence that the "right" thing comes to you, which will lead to all that follows?

The idea to paint the door is a flash of intuition, but it doesn't come from nowhere. It comes from what we've learned about in the last chapter and the chapters before them: full awareness, having the Ego out of the driver's seat, the ability to make a third-level choice that's a non-Ego-driven act of benevolence.

Having the de-coupled mind ready to serve the big YOU is handy, too. As soon as the choice is made to paint the door, the mind immediately swings into support action with a chain of logical thinking: *Okay, paint the man's door; I'll have to buy the paint* — and it comes to a question about a crucial detail, without which the whole enterprise might go wrong. *What color? Better keep this guy talking a little longer, until I find out what color to use.*

Then after that comes the follow-through: bringing the idea into action. That's a lot of work, with more decisions to be made and with more touchy moments to be handled along the way. The same inner condition is needed for those steps.

Consider, for instance, the neighbor's bold stroke of showing up at the house and going right to work on the door, without first telling the owner what he intended to do. That was probably the correct choice. But it carried the risk of appearing and feeling very foolish, if the owner had come storming out and chased him away. The Ego never wants to be the fool. The APE's duty is to shield the Ego from such risks. Thus, an Ego-driven person most likely could not have made the choice the neighbor did. For as we all know, more than once in our lives, each of us has held back from taking an inspired creative step that probably would've worked and posed no actual risk to our well-being or anyone else's, even if it hadn't worked. The only thing that stopped us was the Egoic fear of looking bad.

Finally, a postscript. As far as I know, this true story does not have a happy "ending," at least not yet. What you have read here was more like a happy beginning.

According to the last reports I heard, the reclusive old gentleman had begun to change in a positive way but he still had far to go. For instance, he had opened up to the friendly neighbor, but not yet to other people — and meanwhile the friendly neighbor had duties to attend to in his own life. That friend was reaching the limits of the help he could offer and the time that he could devote. Clearly more steps were needed, including from the old gentleman himself, before one could truly say that a life had been turned around.

While a single creative act can have great impact, instant happy endings are rare. Mostly they happen in fiction. Ebenezer Scrooge goes to bed as a bitter old recluse, and thanks to some visits from supernatural spirits, he wakes up as an enlightened soul brimming with joy and kindness.

Certainly it is possible for any of us to change quickly. Let's not rule that out. The point is, let's also not expect our creativity to work like a magic wand. In most cases a single burst of creative action will take us only part of the way to the goal.

This tends to be especially the case for the goals that matter the most to us. You may come up with a creative birthday surprise that delights your spouse or your significant other, but if the goal is to revive a relationship that has gone stale, you'll probably need an ongoing stream of insights and ideas to open the doors to new ways of relating. Likewise if you set out to write the Great American Novel, the brilliant idea you had for Chapter 1 will be ancient history by the time you face the problems of writing Chapter 3.

In other areas of life as well, accomplishing anything substantial usually calls for *sustained* creativity, which our inner creatures will try to resist. Your Ego will not like being left behind day after day so that you can travel far outside its comfort zone to pursue a more creatively intimate relationship. The APE is going to hate sitting down every day to work on that novel, while the PIG is going to want either instant fame and fortune or a snack from the refrigerator.

Switching perspective from the little you to the big YOU is a good way to jump-start the creative process and stay in it. From the perspective of the little you, overcoming every challenge is a gigantic undertaking, because it's an isolated and lonely little you that's trying to tackle the world. By contrast, the big YOU is in harmony with the world. From that perspective the obstacles, distractions, and resistances that we experience are not nearly as daunting. They are seen as what they are: just a natural part of the process we undergo in order to create.

The message, however, is not that we have to keep our noses to the grindstone. It's more like an invitation to be free of the grindstone — free of the mental routines that have bound and limited us in the past. The invitation is to stop thinking of creativity as a special sort of tool that we pull out for special occasions, and to start seeing it as a natural aspect of our natural selves. It's an invitation to be fully alive by creating our lives as we go along.

A Repeating Cycle, an Expanding Circle

Perhaps the hardest part is understanding that creativity is a cyclical process, full of mid-course corrections, rather than a steady straight-line progression toward a goal. Only an Egoic mind would think that it can march inexorably toward what it wants without making a mistake or experiencing a setback. The Egoic mind is a "narrow" mind because the Ego is a controller. When it takes on projects, it wants those projects to be predictable and controllable — which often leads to predictable, formulaic results. Driving along a road in Seattle once, I saw this quotation on a message board outside a church: "A narrow mind fits neatly in a rut."

Creative activity is adventurous. We are trying to do things we haven't done before, perhaps that no one has done, so we may not hit the mark the first time and may have to try again, a different way. On a long-running project we may even change our notion of what "the mark" is, heading off in a new direction based on what we've learned.

Inventions, works of art, new businesses and other creative works all evolve as they are being created. The book you're now reading was mapped out carefully at the start but it became quite different from the original plan. The original opening is now the beginning of Chapter 3. Since the first draft, many new parts have been added while other parts were dropped, or revised several times. Some chapters, such as this one and the next, include materials and insights that didn't come to my attention until after I had finished the first draft.

For these reasons, the creative process is described as highly "iterative." You begin with a vision of the end result, of course, but from that point it usually is not just a process of laying the foundation and filling in the details, as if you were working from a blueprint. You might keep arriving at new versions of your vision: Vision 2.0, Vision 3.0, maybe more. And even if the final goal is clearly defined, the process is one of "successive approximation," coming gradually closer and closer to your ideal.

Again, the inner creatures don't like this process. They want the job to be done, rewarded, and painless. It is well worth it to move beyond their protests. While some hard work will be required, the journey is one of constant *discovery*. At every stage, we learn and we grow. Often we are astonished, amused, or enlightened by what we discover, both about the world and about ourselves. We come away with a larger appreciation of what the world is, and what we are.

Better yet, creative activity is contagious. Usually the creative circle expands during the process, as other people add in their creativity. Once a playwright writes a new play, the script will be honed during trial readings and performances with actors, who may contribute some of the best material. Start a new business and you'll find yourself hiring people who have ideas you never thought of.

Be creative in your relationship with your partner, and chances are your partner will respond in kind.

The Ego will balk at letting others into the game. After all, you are giving up "creative control," and it is common to hear some monkey-mind chatter about how wrong other people's ideas are. The challenge is to maintain a state of both inner and outer awareness. Then you are open to input from others, while also being able to evaluate someone's idea on the basis of its merit instead of whether it threatens your Ego-identity.

Ultimately, control is a delusion anyway. When you are being highly creative, your projects and ideas will seem to take on "a life of their own," showing you where to go instead of the other way around. And, they will energize others to the point where those people will take hold of them and carry them far beyond anywhere you could go alone.

If you have a computer, think of all the things you can do with it, then let me ask you a question. How often do you use it to do what computers were originally meant to do? They were invented to work out complicated math problems — literally, to compute. All the cool features that have been added since are the results of "follow-on invention." The first clunky computers were barely plugged in and running when vast numbers of people began to pick up the idea and expand upon it.

Today we worry that spending too much time in front of a computer can eat away at our lives, isolating us from physical action and from real-world contact with other people. Although that is something to be watchful about, remember too that this little machine, which can be so addictive if we let it, also represents one of the greatest collective journeys in creativity ever undertaken. I know. I have been part of that journey. The two companies I started and the products that we created were computer-based. Our best known product — a system called MediaSite Live, for recording and sharing rich media presentations — is still widely used, by college professors, trainers, speakers and others making their lectures and courses available online. Thus the expansion of the creative circle goes on, and knowing that one has played a role in such an endeavor is one of the most gratifying rewards there can be.

In the next section, let's briefly review what a number of other people over the years have said and written about creativity. Much of it dovetails closely with what we've learned so far. Then I will suggest some further thoughts, using other examples.

The Classic 'Four Steps'

Creativity comes into play when you have a task before you which cannot be done just by logical problem solving or by learning the how-to steps. You are going to have to make up at least some of it.

In fact, some inventors, when they're envisioning a new product of any kind, will divide the work ahead into two categories. In one category are the parts of their new gadget that they could obviously figure out how to make, or even buy ready-made. In the other category are the unknowns — the parts of the problem that can't be solved by any existing method they know of.

For instance, if your vacuum cleaner at home is fairly new, it's probably a bagless type. It has a lot of pieces that are pretty much standard on all types of vacuum cleaners, but discovering how to make the "bagless" chamber work well for suction and dirt-catching was no easy feat. There were many unknowns to be tackled and it was where the designers had to be truly creative.

Many people who study creativity, along with many who practice it for a living, agree that there are four typical steps in any creative approach. The Englishman Graham Wallas, author of a 1926 book called *The Art of Thought,* is credited with being the first to spell them out:

1. *Preparation.* You begin by studying the problem or project and starting to come at it in a logical manner. Perhaps you read up on the subject, or make some first-stab plans or sketches. Perhaps you ask somebody for advice or just search your own memory to ask, *Have I ever seen anything similar that can tell me what I should do here?*

This step is essentially the kind of "preparation" Louis Pasteur talked about. Using the terms we've developed in this book, we'd say that you are doing it at Level 2 awareness with your logical, thinking mind. Since logically applied thinking will not, by itself, give you the answer you seek, sooner or later you move on to the next step.

2. *Incubation.* Here you turn the problem over to the part of yourself that most people call the subconscious. In our

terms, of course, we don't consider it "sub" to anything: we'd say that you are now operating from your core or natural self, accessing your highest level of awareness. The more "prepared" you are in terms of your inner condition, the quicker you can move to this step!

Graham Wallas believed it was helpful at this stage to stop actively trying to find a solution. He recommended forgetting about the task for a while and going off to do something else. Almost all of us have tried that at some time, though many highly creative people don't find it necessary and will actually keep reflecting on the problem as they go about other business. Either way, you are engaging something beyond or in addition to your thinking-and-trying mind. There is a certain "stillness" — I'll say more about that later — in which ideas can just percolate, or, as Wallas put it, incubate.

3. *Illumination.* This is the Aha or the Eureka! step, when a solution comes to you in what seems to be a flash of inspiration. Maybe the whole thing doesn't come to you at once, but you get an insight into a new way to go about it, one that you hadn't come close to thinking of before.

4. *Verification.* Now you follow through on the idea to verify whether it works. Some people prefer to call this step "refinement," because even if you are on the right track, the step may involve a good bit of tweaking the idea and filling in the details to put it into working form. This is the successive approximation we discussed earlier.

And if your brilliant idea turns out not to work — or if it's only a partial solution, which just accomplishes one part of the task — then you go back to step 1 and keep iterating until you get to where you want to be.

There is no concept of "failure" here. The only failure is to stop short of the goal. That is why so many people credit persistence as the key to their success. Naturally there is such a thing as an impossible goal, like trying to build a perpetual motion machine or turning lead into gold, but success in these cases means having the awareness to recognize when a task is truly impossible ... and then revising your vision to set out on a new path that could be more realistic. We have already discussed that, too. It's just another form of iteration.

The key point is that typically, you don't only go through the four steps once and you're done. You might go through many, many 1-to-4 cycles; you might have multiple cycles running at once on different parts of the job.

But let's devote the rest of this chapter to the step that everybody seems most eager to hear about. That would be the light-bulb Illumination step. People want to know its secrets and how to make it happen; they want to learn how to "think outside the box." This is an amusing phrase, when you consider that *thinking is the box.* Logical, Level-2 thinking is precisely what you need to go outside of, in order to be at Level 3 where you are open to *receiving* an illumination.

You have to get there — or, more accurately, increase your prospects of receiving the illumination — by means other than thinking. Perhaps we can shed some light on what these methods might be.

Making Connections

It's often said that creative insights involve putting things together that don't normally go together, or seeing connections that weren't visible before.

One couple in my city tells of such an incident with their four-year-old. They had taught the child table manners, including proper use of dining utensils: the knife, the fork, and the spoon. Then one day the parents sat down to dinner to find that their daughter had done something odd. She had taped a fork and spoon together by the handles to make a single utensil, with the tines of the fork at one end and the bowl of the spoon at the other.

The girl proudly announced that her "invention" would make it easier to eat, and easier to set the table and clean up. There was no need for the fork and the spoon to be two separate pieces, she explained — because "you never use them both at the same time." If dinnerware sets of the future contain single-piece fork-and-spoons, remember you read it here first.

Now let's see what is behind this type of creative act. Some creativity scholars might explain it by saying that the little girl was fairly new to the whole business of eating with utensils, so she was able to look at the situation with fresh eyes. Since she hadn't been using forks and spoons in the usual way for very long, she was "unencumbered by pre-existing concepts" of them, and hadn't been conditioned to take them for granted as they are.

But that doesn't make much sense in this case. The girl's parents, authority figures whom she trusted and respected, had very explicitly taught her the pre-existing concepts. They had shown and told her what each utensil was for, and modeled how to use each one. They had also held and guided her hands through the motions, and they had complimented her as she made progress in the traditional way. Yet still, she saw another way.

I would suggest a different explanation for the four-year-old and her invention. Whether she knew it or not, when she was learning about dining utensils, she was practicing awareness-based learning. Certainly she was taking in her parents' instructions and trying to follow them, with her thinking mind. But her higher awareness naturally focused on the one thing that matters most when you're eating — picking up food and getting it into your mouth. This, in turn, enabled her to notice something that struck her as silly: the need to keep switching the pick-up utensils for different kinds of food. From that point the creative leap isn't far away. After all, you never use both at the same time!

Perhaps we can clear up a basic bit of confusion about creative insights. Yes, it's true that some great discoveries in various fields of science have been made by newcomers with fresh eyes. And yes, some beautiful art is created by so-called "outsider" artists who never went to art school. Don't underestimate what a beginner can do. But if newness to a field were a *requirement* for having creative insights, then learning wouldn't pay, and we would actually get worse as we gained experience. A child could figure out a tricky problem with your car better than a trained mechanic could, and a musical amateur could write better symphonies than Beethoven. Those things don't happen very frequently.

Most highly creative people find that learning and experience help them to make new connections. Scientists prepare themselves to make discoveries by studying what scientists before them have found. Our four-year-old had to learn the usual way of eating before she could see an opportunity for improvement. What makes the difference for beginners and experts alike is *awareness*.

We are all, to a large degree, creatures of mental habit. Our societies condition us to perceive, think, and act in certain ways. A lot of that conditioning is useful. Yet at the same time it can lock us into habitual patterns, which prevent us from seeing that there are other ways of "putting things together." By being fully aware, we're able to notice this effect. We can be aware of our own conditioning without being bound by it — just as the little girl did — then move beyond it to make connections on another plane.

Switching Perspective

There seems to be an additional factor at work here, though. Doesn't awareness depend on your point of view — on how you look at things?

People also say that creative insights come from changing the frame of reference, or, as I prefer to call it, switching perspective. In books on creativity, this is often illustrated with a drawing that looks like two different things depending on how you look at it, or with a crossword-clue example. What's a seven-letter word for "Tombstone location?" No, it's not "cemetery" (eight letters) or "graveyard" (nine). It's "Arizona," where the famous *town* called Tombstone is located.

The examples are clever. But I prefer to use my little story called The Bird and Fish Argument:

> Once a bird and a fish got into a big argument. They were arguing about a boat. The bird called out, "Look, look! I see a colorful bowl on the water. It's filled with creatures and interesting things." The fish said, "What is 'water'? And besides, I see no colors and no bowl. I just see a big, dark, smooth object hovering above my head, and it doesn't have any opening that things could go into, not even a tiny crack."
>
> "Bowl!" "Dark smooth object!" Unless the fish could soar above the lake to see what the bird sees, and the bird could plunge below the surface and look up, they would never understand or see each other's point of view. Finally they gave up and went their separate ways — while also failing to fully understand what a boat is, and needs to be.

I like this story because it has multiple messages. Perspective isn't only about how you look at it, it's a matter of who is looking. *And the whole picture will elude you unless you see the other person's perspective, then integrate it with yours.* Take note, please, because this is the cause of so many conflicts in the world: Both the bird and the fish saw what they saw, and truthfully reported what they saw — from their *limited* perspectives. Neither one was "wrong" and neither was lying. But neither one could grasp the whole situation, either. A boat is something that's smooth and closed on the bottom, so it can ride the surface of the water, *and* open at the top so it can hold things.

Seeing the viewpoints of others and integrating them with our own is a powerful kind of perspective-switching. Very often it will lead to creative solutions, while neglecting it usually creates nothing but problems.

Have you heard the term "wrap rage"? It's what we feel when we buy products in packaging that can't be opened without tools and weapons, or that can't be re-closed properly after the first use: you grab the spaghetti box from the shelf and a thousand strands of uncooked spaghetti go clattering across the kitchen floor. Too much packaging is designed by people who did not take proper heed of the user's perspective.

On the other hand, I'm looking at a little tube of sunscreen designed with a captive top, the kind that stays attached when you open it. This is done so that when you are on vacation at the lake, you won't accidentally drop the little plastic top over the side of the boat or lose it on the beach ... and a fish or a bird won't be harmed by thinking it's something to eat.

In the design of all sorts of things, the highest creativity comes from integrating and synthesizing the perspectives of everyone involved, from the people who will have to make the product to those who will buy it, repair it or recycle it. Then we get products that are easy to manufacture — and therefore don't cost a lot — as well as easy to sell, use, maintain and dispose.

Conversely, designs that don't work out so well tend to come from a partial or limited perspective. And interestingly, the limited perspective is often one that feeds the Ego of the designer or the user, or both. That's how we get high-fashion clothes that scream "look how creative I am!" but aren't comfortable or practical. Not to mention software and gadgets loaded with features we don't need, and movies that are full of dazzling special effects but don't bother to tell a story that anyone cares about.

Trying to show off one's "creativity" is never as powerful as just seeing things from the perspective of others. The first is a narrow-minded exercising of the Ego. The second requires us to expand our awareness, which therefore expands the creative possibilities.

One catch is that learning and considering other people's perspectives can be much trickier than it seems. The ability to see .things as others see them is an art in itself, and good creators develop that ability. Creative companies like Apple are said to really "understand their customers." Skilled fiction writers, who are able to make up convincing characters and tell moving stories, tend to be keen observers of how people behave and respond in real life.

Certainly all sorts of methods are available for gathering information from people, from market surveys and focus groups to plain old asking questions and listening. But as anyone in the polling business will tell you, the answers you get depend on the questions you ask, as well as on what people feel inclined to say.

Then comes the matter of interpreting what we observe. I can try to read your body language, and by watching your face and posture and noticing things like the tone of your voice, I can think that I understand perfectly how you view a particular situation. Yet if all I'm doing is *projecting my own feelings onto yours*, I could be off by a mile.

You have surely heard of the misunderstandings that can arise in dealing with people from a culture other than your own, such as thinking that someone who won't look you in the eye is being evasive when in fact he is showing respect. Those types of difficulties also arise between people in the same culture, even the same family, for the simple reason that other people are not you or me.

There are common attributes we all share as human beings. To understand others, we must recognize and honor these essential qualities that unite us. The key is not to presume that the other person is just another version of us, standing in separate shoes. Not to presume that just by sharpening up our listening and watching skills, we can literally "put ourselves into the shoes" of others and see the world as they see it, or feel what they are feeling.

True awareness of others starts with self-awareness, inner awareness. By knowing deeply who and what we are, and how we function, we are better able to make the key distinctions — knowing what unites us with those other people, while also being ever alert to what they may see, feel, or know that is radically *different* from anything we might have imagined.

Then, having made the distinctions, we can see how the pieces go together to make a bigger picture. By integrating the other person's perspective with our own we get an enriched, well-rounded, 3-D view of the situation — a view in which we can find creative insights that serve us all.

Which brings us to another important principle.

Creativity Is Always Win-Win

Some people get good at sensing how others think and feel in order to manipulate them. Con artists learn the psychology of their victims. Certain people learn how to push our buttons so they can get what they want.

I would not call that creativity. It doesn't create something new and valuable that can *live*. It's just an Ego game. The Ego is always on the lookout to enhance itself by diminishing others. Using its Ego antenna, it homes in on other people who are, themselves, under the control of their Egos and inner creatures. It tricks their PIGs into jumping at an offer that's too good to be true. It pushes their Egos' guilt buttons until their APEs will do anything to avoid the pain.

In situations like these, the Ego is out to win by making others lose. And win-lose may feel good for a while but it is not sustainable. *Win-lose always degenerates into lose-lose.* Both the victim and the perpetrator lose, over the long run.

Wait a minute, you may say. Some con artists get away with their scams indefinitely, and a certain someone I know has gotten away with pushing other people's buttons for years. Yes, but in doing so, they've also gotten far away from the joy of being in the core or natural self, living as the big YOU. They have closed themselves up in their Ego-caves — funneling endless, priceless energy into scheming how not to get caught, and into trying to draw nourishment from relationships that have shrunk into button-pushing battles. Their Egos are continually fed to maintain a sense of "success" — but in the big picture, they have diminished themselves incalculably and diminished those around them.

That is the opposite of creativity, the opposite of enhancing the world by bringing something new into it.

Creativity is always win-win. And instead of getting drawn into an argument about whether this principle applies in every case you might think of, I would invite you to test the principle in the only way that matters. Try it out for yourself. Try it in the next life situation that comes up.

Here is an example of win-win creativity. Late in his life, Fred Rogers, the creator of the *Mister Rogers* TV show for children, told a magazine reporter a story from his own childhood. Fred was raised in a town about fifty miles from Pittsburgh. On Saturdays, the family would drive to the city to go shopping. The trip took well over an hour, and in those days before DVD players and Nintendos, it was a challenge to keep small children from getting antsy in the car. *What do you give them to do?* Well, young Fred had been given a job that he loved to do as they approached the city.

Pittsburgh at that time was still a steelmaking center, with mills and smokestacks all across the landscape. Fred's father worked for a company that made the special bricks for lining the insides of the furnaces. And Fred's job was to count how many of the smokestacks along the route were smoking. That was a nice measure of how busy the mills were and how many bricks would soon be needed for re-lining, from Dad's company.

A clever Ego trick? Hardly. "My Dad trusted me to count correctly, and he let me know that it mattered," Fred Rogers told the reporter. "Here I am more than 60 years later, and that memory is still as vivid as if it had happened last week."

Everyone wins. The ride is peaceful, Dad gets useful information, the mills are served. And for the child, it's an unforgettable part of growing up to be a responsible, creative adult who will end up serving millions of others.

Synergy vs. Compromise

A win-win result with such wide-ranging impact creates synergy. The whole is more than the sum of its parts, and *everyone* gets more. Synergy is quite different from compromise, in which everyone gets something by agreeing to give up something else. Compromise is a process of satisfying Egos. Each person can walk away believing that he or she got a concession from the other guy that was very important, while sacrificing something that was, ahem, maybe not so important.

Great effort is often put into negotiating compromises that leave all parties' Egos intact. Then the contestants can emerge holding each other's hands aloft and grinning for the TV cameras: *We passed a bill that has something for everybody!* That is considered a "fair deal," but an Ego deal is never an excellent deal. The result is never more than the sum of its parts; it is often dysfunctionally less, and even in the best case, everyone loses at least a little.

When you synergize, you are dealing with more than Ego. Stephen Covey and others who have written on the subject say that reaching synergy requires two conditions. One is "humility" — knowing that your way of seeing things is not the only way. The other is getting down to "core intentions." This means setting aside the specific demands and requests that people have brought to the table, so each can speak of what he or she fundamentally wants — which can often be achieved by doing something that no one, on their own, has considered yet.

It's not hard to see how the process reflects the principles we've been talking about. We are stepping out of the Ego, taking in the other person's perspective, and opening up our awareness to new choices that a larger intelligence may bring.

And stepping out of the Ego is essential. Hazel Henderson, the author of *Building a Win-Win World,* first made her mark as a social activist. She was what you might call a genius at synergy. Time and again she was involved in creating grassroots movements that grew and had impact, despite having few resources. In an interview, Hazel Henderson talked about a lesson she had learned as an organizer:

[When] you're trying to recruit idealistic, wonderful people ... [for] social change organizations where there's no money involved, no motivation of money, it's just a job to be done in terms of an idealized vision of how society could be in the future, you'd better not be so ego-driven as to want to take credit.

These words are from a book called *Creativity,* which was based on in-depth interviews with 91 accomplished creators, from authors like Madeleine L'Engle to leading engineers and scientists.

In many of the interviews the same message resonated again and again: get the Ego out of the way. Dr. Jonas Salk, the developer of the polio vaccine, made it very clear that putting egos aside in order to achieve synergy does *not* mean just meekly sitting back to let others speak their minds. You test and question each other, he said, but you do it in a way that "harmonizes":

> There is a tendency to draw each other out, to bring out the best or the most creative aspect ... In this kind of interaction each person helps the others see what they see. That's what is needed in the world today to reconcile differences, resolve conflicts, help us each understand what our belief systems represent ...

The *Creativity* book was compiled and written by the Hungarian psychologist Mihaly Csikszentmihalyi. Near the end of the book, Mihaly himself summed up what appears to be needed for *any* kind of creativity — alone or in groups, in personal life or in a profession. He said the first task for many of us is simply freeing up the "psychic energy" and attention required: "In a person concerned with protecting his or her self, practically all the attention is invested in monitoring threats to the ego." And likewise "for some people the concept of 'need' is inflated to the point that it becomes an obsession ... When everything a person sees, thinks, or does must serve self-interest, there is no attention left over" for creativity.

Mihaly's book was published in 1996. I didn't come across it until long after starting this book. It was an interesting confirmation to find the Ego mentioned by so many others as an obstacle to creativity. And, in the passage quoted above, it was downright remarkable to find such a distinct foreshadowing of what we're now calling the Ego's minions — the APE and the PIG — along with repeated emphasis on "attention," or what we are here calling awareness.

Stillness

In closing this chapter let's follow up on an earlier note about the "Incubation" stage of the creative process. This is the stage in which you have done a lot of your thinking-mind homework and you're hoping for "Illumination." I had mentioned a certain quality that's needed in order to be open to illumination.

That key quality is *stillness*. And it is not necessary to actually sit still in a meditative posture in a quiet room. Prominent creative people have reported aha illuminations coming to them while they were out and about in the streets, or taking a bath, or doing countless other things.

Stillness means your mind is still, in the sense that it's not messing with you. The mind may well be doing some of the thinking and processing that make up its everyday business. It may indeed be thinking about the very subject on which you'd like to be illuminated — but it is *not* filled with the noise and the monkey-mind chatter that would interfere with your ability to access higher levels of intelligence. You are ready to receive illumination, but not distracted by the PIG squealing *Ooh, my master the Ego must have the answer right now,* or by APE fears like *What will happen if I don't get the answer?*

Here was Isaac Newton describing his process of discovery:

> I keep the subject constantly before me, and wait till the first dawnings open slowly, by little and little, into the full and clear light.

That is beautiful. It describes a state of being that has been called by many names, such as focused awareness, or calm alertness.

Was Isaac Newton a perfect Zen master of quieting the mind, a silent and beatific saint in all that he did throughout his life? From the records we have, not exactly. However I would mention, as many have, that striving for enlightened perfection can become a distracting Ego goal in its own right. The state that Newton achieved, which we can trust to be sufficient for any need, is a state available to any of us: the stillness to receive illuminations one by one.

Final Thoughts: Motivation and Joy

Of course, creativity is not all quietude and stillness and waiting. There are moments of great exuberance. Do you dance? We all do, if only in private. Scientists dance around the laboratory when they make a discovery — Newton probably did — and dance may be the most ancient of the arts. It is quite possible that in primeval times, our human ancestors danced long before they could sing, before they had language.

Yet as we've seen, creativity in any field, including dance, if you choose to get serious about that field, is also hard work. It places high demands upon every one of our faculties. It requires practice and persistence. There are plenty of moments that don't feel much like fun.

Despite how taxing creative work can be, many people devote themselves to it passionately, even amateur artists and after-hours inventors. Why do they do it? In fact, questions are often raised about what motivates us humans to be creative. It's been said that necessity is the mother of invention, but in countless cases necessity is not a factor.

What makes people tinker long into the night, night after night, with an idea for an invention or a book that nobody ever said they needed? Why do people spend hours at the computer editing their home videos and digital photos, not only neglecting what they really need to do, but neglecting their usual time-wasting pastimes on the Internet? And what about those who walk away from a solid career path to go off on some creative tangent that seems, well, not so solid?

Maybe for some the goal is fame and fortune, or at least the pride of being recognized as a creative type. Yet many artists and creators who have achieved fame and fortune have said — and many studies have confirmed — that while these rewards are nice, they're the wrong ones to use as motivators. One problem is that when you're out for glory, your creative output is not likely to be very creative. Among other things, you become a people-pleaser: pandering to the audience, trying to impress the critics, trying to write a best-seller by following that surefire formula that will give them what they want. In his book *The War of Art,* the author Steven Pressfield calls this type of writer "the definition of a hack."

People-pleasing behavior comes from an Ego craving reassurance and attention. It produces something that's either predictable or crassly sensational, and it is not the same as serving others creatively by giving them something genuinely "new and valuable." Accomplishing that is a lot harder. It's more like work.

So what is the genuine reason, the healthier and higher motivation, for doing creative work? Steven Pressfield's simple answer is, "for its own sake." Others simply say they love the work, or feel called to it. Even in the taxing or uncomfortable moments, they feel fully alive and engaged — which is not surprising for an activity through which one can give to others, while giving oneself a life that becomes a journey of discovery.

Creativity scholars have technical terms for summing up all of this. As the Harvard professor Teresa Amabile writes, "intrinsic motivation" — doing the work for the rewards inherent in doing it — is powerful, while "extrinsic motivation," doing the work for some other reason, such as what one can get for doing it, is detrimental.

And there is a three-letter word that sums up what people intrinsically find in creative activity. As we'll see in the last chapter, it is a reward intrinsic to life itself, and available in every moment of life: joy.

Chapter 9
THE STATE OF JOY

As the sage said long ago, to every thing, there is a time. Life is a roller coaster, not only full of highs and lows, but always changing in the kinds of situations it presents.

There will be times when we have a chance to be creative and times when we need to follow a prescribed routine. There will be days when we can go about the business in front of us knowing that everything else is in hand, at least for the time being, and days lived amid high uncertainty: *What will the test results say? How is that other thing working out? Should I even be doing this right now; should I have done what I just did?*

Ideally, we would like to savor every minute of this life. Have you ever watched people coming out of a roller coaster ride at the end? When it is time to move on from this life, we would like to be one of the people who come out beaming and eager for what's next, not one who comes out with a look that says the ride was an agony.

And the quality of our experience will depend on our inner state. If we resent the routines in our lives or find them boring, while also dreading the uncertainties and letting them make us sick with worry, that's a miserable state. It leaves us room to be happy only at the occasional times when conditions are just right.

To improve the quality of our lives, we can try to learn coping skills. We can set out to "make the best" of each unwanted situation and try not to worry so much. The trouble with this state is, it's still based on seeing life as an enemy. Life is still perceived as an unreliable thing we are "in," which, instead of arranging itself to suit us, often surrounds us with problems and ordeals. So we roll out the strategies: changing what we can, and adjusting our inner attitudes so as to look for silver linings and not let the other stuff "get to us."

While this is more helpful than resenting and worrying, we can go vastly further. We can make a more fundamental adjustment, to help us truly experience the journey and revel in it. The adjustment starts with simply seeing that we are not our Egos.

As soon as we recognize that we are not our Egos, we detach ourselves from the primary inner source of *un*happiness in our lives. The rest of the trip — the road to joy, or more accurately, the road *of* joy — then becomes a lot easier.

To grasp why this is so, let's review some things we have learned. We'll be taking it slowly, while adding a new twist that may shed some additional light.

The Source of Unhappiness and Suffering

Here is the core of the problem. We've learned that the Ego is a delusion. It is a mind-made identity, a fictional version of ourselves, fabricated by the mind. And like any delusion or fabrication, the Ego isn't really "alive."

This Ego, this fictional you or me, is actually no more alive than a fictional character in a novel or a comic strip. It isn't connected to life, and it doesn't partake of the life of the universe in the way that genuine living beings do.

The Ego can only be "kept alive" as a sort of parasite, by hijacking and coupling with its creator, the thinking mind. However ...

Once the Ego is firmly coupled with the thinking mind, it becomes a very powerful delusion that persists — because we're always thinking! We then proceed to live delusionally. The mind is constantly "narrating the story" of this fictional identity that isn't really us, interpreting everything that actually happens through the eyes of the Ego. And while the details vary, the basic nature of the story is always the same.

Not being truly alive, *the Ego sees itself as a separate identity operating "in" life, like a lonesome soldier in enemy territory.* To the Ego, every task is a battle to be won or lost, just as every interaction with another human being is an "encounter." Everything that exists in the world — even one's own body! — is perceived either as something to be conquered and mastered, or as something to be feared and hated.

If you don't believe it, stop and reflect. You've heard the Egoic mind-chatter a million times. It is the perpetual voice-over to the delusional movie, and it says things like *This job is stupid. I'm surrounded by jerks. The whole society is screwed up.* You try to prevail, but the very forces of nature are against you: *There's never enough time.* Your mind may even tell you that *It's a jungle out there* — as if a jungle were a bad thing, not a natural thing. There are times you exult because, ha ha, despite the odds, you're winning ... but then it's no, wait, now you're losing ... and so it goes, through a never-ending series of skirmishes.

No wonder we get so exhausted! In order to exist at all, the Ego constantly needs to assert and defend itself. It's constantly wanting to be rewarded and recognized, satisfied and gratified. Whenever that isn't possible — which is often — it wants to be soothed with sympathy, or justified with righteous indignation. Keeping the Ego on life support is a burden that can wear out the most energetic person.

No wonder so many of us become so frustrated, when all that we ever "really wanted" from life was just to "be happy." But here is where another pitfall looms.

The Trouble with 'I Want to Be Happy' — and the Simpler Solution

"I want to be happy" sounds like the most natural of all human desires. It was the goal that I set out to achieve for myself after my unhappy early years, many years ago. However, you may have heard that trying to be happy is not the way to be happy — and the reason is, it's typically just another Ego goal.

How could it possibly be an Ego goal? Well, we know that our own words can trip us up if we're not clear about what they really mean, when we use them. Furthermore, our thinking mind tends to think in words. And the very thought that our mind phrases as "I want to be happy" leaves a basic confusion unresolved: who is the "I"? It's usually the voice of the Ego, the ever-demanding Ego, that is saying "I want to be happy."

We then are faced with a choice. We can choose to *be* happy ... or we can set about trying to make the Ego happy. Many self-improvement programs that we undertake wind up being the latter. The Ego goal becomes an Ego project. We've got endless tweaking and remodeling under way, both on the exterior and on the interior of ourselves, with the aim of upgrading our condition. But as long as we are imprisoned in the Ego cave that we read about in Chapter 5, our efforts will come down to little more than renovating the cave, trying to make it a more pleasant and secure stronghold in the battlefield of life.

There is a simpler and more direct route, leading to an immensely greater happiness. It is to step away from the cave and embrace life, instead of trying to conquer it or control some little corner of it. It is to realize that we are not only "in" life, we *are* life.

This is the most profound realization there can be. And it is quite different from some intellectual exercise in "stepping outside yourself" to get a more objective view. It is stepping into yourself, into the big YOU, to be who you are.

"To be or not to be, that is the question" indeed!

Simply to be who we are, and to know what we are, is to be in the state of joy.

Stories of Realization and Joy

Many people throughout history, from ancient mystics to modern-day working people, have given us written accounts of coming to this realization. A story often re-told is that of Chiyono, who lived in China in the thirteenth century and was one of the first women to become known as a great Zen master.

When Chiyono was young she studied and meditated diligently, but she could find neither wisdom nor peace. Then one night she went to fetch water in a wooden pail. It was an old pail that she had repaired many times, bound together with strips of bamboo. She filled it to the brim. She began to carry it along, lurching with the weight, when the bamboo broke. The bottom fell out of the pail. The water rushed out, the weight dropped away — and in that moment Chiyono was "enlightened," liberated, set free.

Reading the story through the lens of this book, we would say that Chiyono was released from her Ego. She realized that for many years she had been doing what many of us do, needlessly. We labor through life, lugging around a mind-constructed identity that we keep patching and fixing while we fill it with stuff that it wants. Life, like water, is precious, but it cannot be contained or possessed in such an unsound vessel. When the bottom dropped out, this woman realized the folly of trying to "hold it together" and allowed herself to be flooded with joy.

Others have spoken of the great realization coming to them at seemingly random moments, not triggered by any symbolic event. Many, too, have tried to describe the state of joy they experienced. Although the accounts differ, and some simply call it a joy beyond words, certain qualities are mentioned again and again in descriptions of this state.

The first quality is extreme awareness. People write of their eyes, ears and senses being opened to the world around them, enabling them to be present to its beauty as never before. For the Irish poet George Russell even the air became visible:

> The winds were sparkling and diamond clear, and yet full of color as an opal, as they glittered through the valley, and I knew the Golden Age was all about me, and it was we who had been blind to it.

People in this state of joy marvel at manmade objects as well as those of nature. The bland skyscrapers of a city on a misty day seem more wonderful than the emerald towers of Oz — more wonderful because one knows that they are real towers, built and inhabited by actual humans.

This leads us to the second quality of the state of joy: knowing that the world is filled with life and that we are intimately connected with that life. For instance, a man I know told me of the following incident. Riding a crowded bus at rush hour on a hot day, he was trying to forget his discomfort by, as he says, "playing a little mind-game. I was looking at the other passengers and telling myself I ought to be grateful that at least I'm not as fat and sweaty as that guy jammed into the aisle, or as old and decrepit as that old lady over there." Then suddenly, in a flash, the Ego game dissolved. The man was amazed to feel his eyes brimming with tears of joy and gratitude for an infinitely larger gift — "just the gift of being in that space and that slice of time with so many of my fellow creatures, all sharing the same life that I do. If I could have found my voice I would have shouted it out: 'This bus is a miracle! You're all so beautiful!' I have never forgotten that."

The third quality of the state of the joy comes naturally with the first two. Alan Watts captured it in his famous essay on joy and enlightenment called "This Is It." In that state, he wrote, we are filled with an assurance that goes beyond any mere feelings of confidence or comfort. Instead we are struck by

a vivid and overwhelming certainty that the universe, precisely as it is at this moment, as a whole and in every one of one of its parts, is so completely *right* as to need no explanation.

The fourth and final quality of joy could be seen as perhaps the most magical. Not only do we step away from the Ego, we transcend our sense of individuality. We seem to merge with everything — while, at the same time, knowing that it's not an illusion. Rather, the old and limited sense of individuality, the sense of being *separate,* was the illusion!

"A human being is a part of the whole," wrote Albert Einstein. "He experiences himself, his thoughts and feelings as something separate from the rest" — but that perception, said Einstein, is only "a kind of optical delusion of his consciousness." Alan Watts put a slightly different twist on it. When we are joyfully enlightened, he wrote, we recognize that our "individual consciousness and existence" is nothing more than "a point of view temporarily adopted by something immeasurably greater."

One Morning's Adventure

As I was completing the work on this chapter, I felt I had collected plenty of research, both from reading and from my own experience and personal contacts. But sometimes the world has a way of telling you that you're not done. A woman in the audience at a talk that I'd just given came up to me afterward, urging me to read one more book.

Wow. In that book, published in 2008, I found a story which must be passed along. The story pulls together what we've learned so far about the state of joy and gives us a perfect bridge to what remains: namely, learning how to realize joy in our daily lives.

The author was alone in her apartment one morning when the realization came to her quite unexpectedly, washing through her in waves, as it were:

"The essence of my being became enfolded in a deep inner peace," she wrote. Anxiety and insecurity vanished, replaced by "the feelings of tranquility, safety, blessedness, euphoria."

Her awareness, and her sense of herself, expanded immensely: "My perception was released from its attachment to categorization and detail ... It was clear to me that this body functioned like a portal through which the energy of who I am can be beamed into three-dimensional space ... the boundaries of my earthly body dissolved and I melted into the universe."

She realized that "for all these years I really had been a *figment of my own imagination.*" And now she felt "like a genie liberated from a bottle."

If you have read the book, you know that this is from *My Stroke of Insight* by Jill Bolte Taylor. You also know the irony of the situation, which is that Dr. Taylor is a brain scientist — and that these realizations, bringing her to this state of joy, washed through her as her own brain was in the process of suffering a massive stroke.

She was being liberated at great peril. The stroke was attacking the centers of logic and language in her left brain, shutting down the thinking-mind functions that the Ego uses to maintain its identity. It even altered her sense of time, eating away at the mind's tendency to obsess about the past or the future: "every moment seemed to exist in perfect isolation" and she was able to be present in each. Luckily, before too many moments had passed, her high state of awareness let her know she was having a stroke that put her in mortal danger. The problem was that the attack on her logical functions also attacked her capacity to respond. Her mind wasn't just de-coupled from her Ego; it was fast becoming disabled.

As the "boundaries" of her body melted away, so did her brain's motor control over the body. Reeling and dragging, she finally made it to the phone, only to face another dilemma. The ability to understand and use words and numbers had faded. This loss had liberated her from the Egoic tendency to label, judge and measure everything, leading to that ineffable state of joy "beyond words," but it was no help at all if one needed to punch numbers into a keypad and then talk to whoever picked up: the keypad looked like gibberish.

Jill Bolte Taylor was very fortunate. Somehow she managed to call a number at her lab. A friend recognized her voice despite her woofing and warbling attempts to say words. Help came in time, and though the stroke would render her immobile for days, she eventually recovered.

Out of the many stories about the state of joy, this one is especially useful because it illustrates a common challenge we all face. Most of us know that it is *possible* to experience profound joy. We have felt it come upon us at random times — maybe not as dramatically as it did for Dr. Taylor, but on certain occasions, for all-too-brief periods, we have been filled with joy and peace. The challenge is to have this state be more than a random and fleeting gift.

We would like to "know joy" in more than the sense of knowing somebody who crosses our path on the street once in a while. We'd like it to be a regular companion. And this, in turn, requires two things. We need to be able to enter the state of joy at any moment — as opposed to just having it pay us a surprise visit — and we need to be able to function in it.

Granted, we usually won't be in the process of being disabled by a stroke. But there will still be many times when we can't afford to slip into a trance-like condition, either. We can't live in the world as if it were our private meditation lounge, constantly saying *Ohhh, man, everything is perfect and I don't need to do anything, so I can just sit here and bliss out while I watch the cosmic fireworks.*

Some of us have tried that route with drugs and it doesn't work very well. It's actually a retreat into the Ego cave, whereas what we're looking for is a step forward, into ... into what?

Into the very ground of joy, which is presence.

Presence

After Jill Taylor had survived her stroke, she didn't want the joy that she had experienced to become a one-time memory, ever more distant in the rearview mirror. She, too, sought the ability to access the state at any time. I agree totally with her discovery:

> Deep inner peace is just a thought or a feeling away. To experience peace does not mean that your life is always blissful. It means that you are capable of tapping into a blissful state of mind amidst the normal chaos of a hectic life.

And how do you tap in? Here again, I agree with her when she says "Step one ... is the willingness to be present in the right here, right now."

The *willingness* to be present. What does that mean? Does it mean we exert "will power" in order to command ourselves to Be Here Now, in capital letters? Not at all.

What is commonly called will power usually comes from the Ego. As we've learned in this book, the Ego and its minions, the PIG and the APE, like to issue urgent commands. They rule by authority and they demand what they want right now — so they can get something out of it.

But commanding yourself to be present right now, in order to get something out of it right now, won't produce the result. Like all Ego projects, this one is self-defeating from the start. You've already put your attention onto something other than being present. You've put it onto the benefits you expect from doing it, and onto the urgency of monitoring whether you are doing it right — *Is this it, have I got it, what if I don't, ARE WE THERE YET?* — all of which will only prevent you from being present.

Presence lives in the opposite direction, away from commanding and demanding, away from the Ego's desires and judgments. And the path to presence is simple. All we have to be "willing" to do is let go of what's keeping us from being present in the first place.

The Amazing Power of Suspended Judgment

To be fully present, we need to be willing to suspend judgment. The biggest obstacle is the automatic habit of constantly judging and evaluating. As one friend of mine puts it, we have a "good-bad meter" in our head that's running most of the time. We either like or don't like what's going on, we agree or disagree with the people around us, we think we're doing OK or not, and so forth. This can prevent us from being present — and in a state of joy — in several ways.

For one thing, if we don't like what's going on, right off the bat we are upset. Maybe we think it's unfair, or we are insulted. Remember the story about my son that I told in Chapter 7, when he said he was offended by something, then quickly corrected himself to say "No, my Ego is offended"? Being upset or offended is a choice, and it is the Ego's choice to react that way. The good-bad meter belongs to the Ego. Its control panel is full of buttons waiting to be pushed. Any one of them will tilt the reading to *bad, bad!*, instantly short-circuiting our chance to be in a state of joy.

Furthermore, the constant automatic judging pulls us out of the present in both time and place. If we judge a situation to be one that we don't like, the mind is quickly filled with APE-chatter about how to get away from this unpleasant experience. If we *do* like the situation, the PIG immediately wants to milk it for all that it's worth. For instance, maybe we're thinking about how to impress this cool person we've just met. The possibilities for such distraction are endless, the Ego and its minions will find them, and they pull us out of simply being here and now.

Finally, as we have seen repeatedly in previous chapters, the judging and evaluating can lead to snap decisions and reflex reactions that lead us further astray. We lash out and make a nasty remark we wish we hadn't. Or we PIG-ishly overreact to a nice

Ego-feeding opportunity, rambling on about our favorite topic until we can no longer help but notice the signs we had missed because we weren't present: the unmistakable body-language signs from others that say "Would somebody please change the channel?" Now people are squirming and wondering how *they* can get away from *us*.

All this may sound like a bunch of negative warnings. But again, the message is that we don't need to undertake any supreme exertions in order to be supremely present in the moment. And we certainly don't need to go chasing joy in order to be in a state of joy. It is our natural state. It's right here. All we need to do is let go of what's stopping or distracting us.

For my friend, what worked was simply being aware that whenever he felt the tensions rising, it was time to unplug the good-bad meter. After a while, he says, he got so used to being without it that much of the time, it "stayed turned off" on its own. He was learning, in an awareness-based fashion, that he didn't need it.

For me, one thing that works is the metaphor of the "third bucket." When I become aware that my Ego is busy sorting the entire flow of experience into either the Good bucket or the Bad bucket, I pull out my third bucket: the bucket called Just Is.

The Just Is bucket is the judgment-suspended bucket, and I can literally hang it under the faucet — *suspend* it under the faucet — to catch the flow of experience without any pre-sorting. Sometimes I use a rhyming pun to remind myself that no matter what's happening, I can do "justice" to it by seeing that it Just Is.

Suspending judgment does not mean abandoning judgment. On the contrary! By suspending judgment, for the moment, we give ourselves time to deliberate and reflect. That will often enable us to make a wiser judgment in a little while, instead of making the snap judgments that get us in trouble — or that drain the joy out of an occasion by making us hostile to it from the start.

When needed, we'll find that we can move from suspension to action very quickly. In cases like those where a child is about to do something disastrous, some people are liable to make things worse by screaming and startling the kid, whereas others seem able to step right in and make the move that saves the day. At the times when you make it worse, you are reacting from the fear and anger of a snap judgment that says "Bad!" When you save the day you are seeing, and responding to, what Just Is.

Finally, suspending judgment means easing up on the tendency to be always snap-judging ourselves. For some of us, here's how perverse it can be: not only are we constantly judging ourselves, we're constantly *judging the fact that we're judging ourselves.* At every little failure we slap ourselves in the head and say *Bad girl!,* then follow up with another slap that says *Bad, BAD girl! You'll never get better if you're so self-critical!*

There's no joy in that. It also doesn't allow us to act effectively, since our attention is focused on beating ourselves up instead of on seeing how to overcome the mistake. So how does one get free of such a negative feedback loop?

Not by making a project out of it — that is, a project that's going to be graded — but simply by being present, in each moment.

We think we just goofed up? Okay, then we can be present to the consequences of the goof. Like the basketball player who takes a poor shot — and doesn't even have time to follow it up with a self-head-slap, because from the moment she lets go of the ball, she's "following the shot" to catch the rebound in case it misses. And if the goof wasn't really a goof? Well, if the shot should go in, then she's moving to get ready for the next play. She is ever present to what Just Is.

The game may not come easy and she won't always win, but the game is *joyful*.

And so it is with being present to our inner selves. Ever present and alert, we notice the APE acting up, or we hear a voice and know it's the voice of the Ego. No need to judge. Like a window-shopper at the mind's window, we are "Just looking, thank you!" And sooner or later, if we keep this up, we notice something that's blatantly obvious but truly marvelous. *There is somebody doing the looking.*

Yep. That looker is the big YOU, the natural "self." It's part of the larger intelligence, the "something immeasurably greater" than the cramped and limited "optical delusion" we thought we were. Aha! Like the genie out of the bottle, we're free. Free to choose, and to see what the choices are. Free to *be* what we are.

This freedom is so absolutely remarkable that it may strike us as absolutely hilarious, the way a good joke does when it cuts to the heart of the matter and we laugh and say Oh, that's *perfect*. Joy is the perfectly simple matter of knowing what we are, and what is.

Moreover, once we see other people "just as they are," we are able to deal with them just as they are. Being fully present and aware, we don't react to people or try to figure them out. Instead, we respond and connect. We even know what to connect with, for we learn to see the twin aspects of other people: their Egos, and their core or natural selves. By making the distinction we're able to look past the Egos, which are mostly interested in doing battle with our own Egos, anyway, and home in on the deep connection. Often we can then "harmonize" with others, as Jonas Salk described in the last chapter, converging on a joint discovery beyond what any of us would have thought possible. This game also is joyful.

Building and Shedding Habits

The state of joy can be cultivated. As we learn to let go and practice being present, not only do we live more and more frequently in the state of joy, we find that it begins to deepen and expand. This may not happen in a straight-line progression, with every state topping the one before until we are radiating high-intensity joy as reliably as the sunshine. But if we remain alert and watchful, from time to time we may reflect and notice that our "quality of life" has been enriched substantially.

We are on the way to building lasting happiness, and it is gradually becoming a happiness that builds upon itself. This is quite distinct from chasing temporary pleasures or pursuing Ego goals, both of which will leave us ultimately unfulfilled, and often call for an increasing effort just to get the same boost we did last time.

When our joy begins to deepen and expand, we know that a couple of things are happening in tandem. They might be called acquiring habit and mastery. In other words, we are growing "accustomed" to living in joy — it's becoming a custom rather than a special occasion — and we are growing more intuitively adept at living within this state.

Are there ways we can help the process along? I will suggest two that I am aware of.

One is just to knowingly practice what works for us. Eckhart Tolle suggests that paying close attention to a single breath can bring about presence, while others find that certain activities in their lives are particularly conducive to being present. For Jill Bolte Taylor, it's walking in the rain. Mine is similar but not weather-dependent: standing in the shower. Perhaps there is something essential about water that brings us into the here and now. It can't be a coincidence that so many people sing in the shower, or that so many children, who aren't as worried about getting their clothes wet as adults are, love to go out and frolic in the rain.

The only practical step I need to take in order to practice my "presence activity" is allowing enough time, so I don't have to shower in a hurry. Whatever yours may be, any such practical step that's required is well worth taking, and the activity itself is well worth the time devoted to it. It restores, refreshes and enhances the healthiest habit there can be, the habit of being present and joyful.

That suggestion should be fairly easy to take. The flip side, shedding unhealthy habits, is what many of us find harder. Unhealthy habits include *but are not limited to* those that are physically unhealthy, such as smoking or overeating. Any habit that interferes with being present and joyful is unhealthy. So start with a question. This is a question to hold in your awareness as you go through life:

What keeps you away from, or takes you out of, the state of joy?

The only rule is, no answers like "It takes me out of the state of joy when my boyfriend chews with his mouth open." That is another person's behavior, for which the question to you is, how do you respond? You are on the lookout for patterns that you repeat, which bring you down, whether they are patterns of thinking or involve physical behavior as well.

These habits can drag you back to the joyless state. Insidiously, they also undermine the practice of being present and aware, which means that the farther back you are dragged the less you notice it, or care to notice. The result is a vicious cycle — one that makes itself ever harder to pull out of — or a slippery slope. That is how we regress, relapse, backslide.

Or, if your state of joy is still tenuous and fragile, these habits can keep you stuck on square one. You may never really begin establishing the new habits that are in accord with being present and joyful.

So how do we break the vicious cycle? The way, as always, is to start from awareness. The way not to proceed, as always, is trying to change a habit by making it an Ego project based on an Ego goal.

Take exercise or weight loss as an example. One reason people fail to *consistently* exercise more, eat less, or both is that they are doing it for an Ego goal — typically, to look good. There are a couple of problems with this. First, in many cases, the goal is specific and temporary: we need to look good for the beach, or for the wedding party. Establishing an ongoing healthy habit isn't even part of the plan. In that case the result is just a crash diet, which may succeed but often doesn't, and then the whole thing slides off the radar until the next big occasion comes up and the Ego says it's time to do it again.

But more fundamentally, an Ego project of this type is apt to fail because it immediately becomes a have-to. Remember, the Ego rules by command and demand: my Ego says I *have to* lose weight. That produces urgency for the result. Choices are then made from urgency, rather than from awareness of what is likely to work for us, and we get frustrated at the slightest sign that we're not doing well enough. The more have-tos we have in our life, the less happy we will be ... and the less happy, the more likely to go off course or give up. Just another vicious cycle, another slippery slope.

This is a perfect case for awareness-based learning. Simply being aware of what's going on with ourselves, both internally and externally, is the start. Out of this awareness, a new habit or the desire for a new habit can then begin to emerge. It emerges from our core self, from knowing what we are and seeing what is appropriate to what we are. Its emergence is guided by the larger intelligence that we are now able to access, rather than by orders from the Egoic commander.

The new habit comes from *being* in joy, and it reinforces that joy — a positive cycle, not a vicious one — rather than from *doing* what we are trying to force ourselves to do. And the old habit, the unhealthy one? We don't have to kick it or break it. We shed it, like a skin we've outgrown. In all these respects, awareness is superior to making a project out of "I need to change my habits."

About Boredom

Speaking of recurring patterns: what if we're just bored? Depending on how bored you feel you are, and what you feel bored with, boredom could be simply a sign that it's time for a change or a sign of serious trouble.

Boredom is very common, yet it's an elusive subject to talk about. How do you even define it, when it doesn't seem to be a "thing" but rather the lack or absence of something, like, "lack of interest" maybe?

In fact we could say boredom is the lack of something that is essential to joy: the lack of engagement and connection. When we are bored, we can't engage or connect with a life situation that we find ourselves in. We feel the activity is beneath us, or of no use; or we've been at it a long time and there seems to be nothing further that we can learn, or enjoy, or accomplish. In short, there's nothing "of interest" to us.

Boredom can feel like the mental equivalent of an empty stomach: the mind growls for something to digest. If the emptiness persists it can leave us feeling enervated, starved of our strength and vigor, weak and listless, falling asleep. Or it may drive us searching for something to do, anything, including sabotage. When a dog left alone in a house chews up the curtains and the furniture, he's confirming the observation of many dog trainers that "a bored dog is a destructive dog." Likewise, a bored mind is a destructive mind. Feeling trapped in a barren cage, the mind is liable to chew at whatever's around. It is literally wasting its time laying waste.

To help see how destructive boredom can be, consider another analogy. It's been said that the opposite of love is not hate, but indifference: the absence of caring at all. Likewise the opposite of joy is not sorrow, but apathy. Joy and sorrow are parts of the same passion for life. When we "invest" in life by being fully present to it, we get joy but also run the risk of feeling deeply sorrowful at times. The two can even show up together at the same time — as when we cry tears of joy! But in a state of apathy, we're not invested in life at all. We haven't got a penny in the joy market. We're so bored we might even be "bored to tears," except that without the joy the tears are empty tears, cried out of nothingness.

So, what are you bored with? If you are bored with all of life, or with a lot of it on most days, that's an unhealthy sign and it is advisable to seek personal or professional help. To climb out of a big hole, a person needs a hand. Start by calling on someone you can trust. Connect and re-connect until you reclaim the high ground, in the state of joy.

Then there are the cases in which we seem to have a specific boredom zone in our lives. We're mainly bored when we are in a particular "Life Space," such as our work or a relationship. The temptation is to blame the situation, and jump directly to finding a new job or new partner that won't be so boring. And, a move of that type may ultimately be the healthy choice. A dog is by nature an outdoor pack animal, and just as a dog may have a hard time flourishing and being itself in an empty house, there may be an environment in your life that isn't suited to the person you are. It may be healthier for all concerned if you find another.

But first it's advisable to reflect on a question. Is it possible that your own inner creatures are part of the problem? For instance, when you're in this particular life situation — whether it's at work, with your partner, or just being alone with yourself — is it possible that your Ego tends to be the one in the driver's seat, and it's actually your Ego that is bored?

After all, the Ego is very easily bored. An Ego is only interested in scenes in which the Ego can flourish, and its minions are pretty restless creatures, too. Once the PIG has rooted up all of the instant Ego-food for its master that it can find, it wants to go scooting off to the grass in the next field on its little PIG legs in order to root for more. The APE will second the motion by howling *Let's get out of here! This is borrr-ing!*

Should that be what's been happening inside you, a change of environment may not be the solution. If the problem is in your cell phone, walking around won't improve the signal.

Certainly it pays to check out this possibility. Through awareness of our inner state, we can discern whether Ego interference is the main source of the disconnect called boredom. Then we're better equipped to make any needed adjustments, so that we can have crystal-clear reception ... and have joyful conversations with life wherever we go.

Ego Goals vs. Non-Ego Goals: Some All-Around Guidelines to Joy

A key message of this chapter is that we cannot find profound joy by pursuing Ego goals. As we've seen in the passages on boredom, weight loss, and other subjects throughout the book, the Ego's agenda is not ours. It will set unhealthy or inappropriate goals and it has unhealthy ways of going after them.

In any such pursuit, only two outcomes are possible:

> ➤ If the Ego goal is met, it will bring Ego gratification — but not joy. All you get is a cheesy artificial substitute for joy, and it doesn't last.

> ➤ If the Ego goal is *not* met, then the hunt is a failure and you feel worse than before.

Either way, you never find the real cheese.

Thus the general rule is, "Don't squander your energy chasing Ego goals." The catch is, the distinction between Ego goals and those that aren't can be elusive and hazy. We are constantly setting and pursuing goals in life, whether it's through a formal goal-setting process or on a moment-to-moment basis, as we choose which motivation to follow at a given time. And the operation is always susceptible to being hijacked.

The Ego, when coupled with the thinking mind, can do a very clever job of persuading us that our motives are noble and pure when in fact the hidden agenda is pure Ego gratification. It can be fairly easy to spot other people who are self-deluded in this way — we call them by labels like "hypocrites." But our own hidden Ego agendas are harder to see, because they're hidden from *us*. Add in the PIG and the APE pushing their master's agenda with extreme urgency, and we can be off track before we know it.

In Chapter 6 we saw how important it is to be aware of what's driving us. Building from that chapter, and borrowing a few things from other chapters as well, we can arrive at a series of guidelines for keeping ourselves on track.

Each of the following is a simple test we can apply, to tell whether we're being driven by Ego goals or by the healthy kind that will bring us joy and lasting fulfillment.

➤ *Who benefits?* If only you do, most likely it's an Ego goal. Joy, like creativity, is always win-win. Others are uplifted by our being in a state of joy, and thus they benefit from whatever will bring us into that state. On the other hand, if we're merely seeking pleasure that won't benefit anyone else, that might be Ego. And if we are building ourselves up at the expense of others, that's definitely Ego.

➤ *Look at the diagram on the next page. It's a copy of "Witnessing the Egoic Mind" from Chapter 5. Can your motivation be found in the list of items under "Your Egoic Self"?* If it's any of those, it's Ego, and what your Ego is driving you to do will not bring joy.

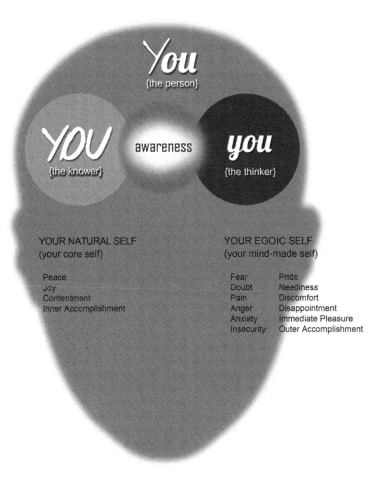

> ➤ *The pursuit of an Ego goal often feels urgent, frantic and frenzied.* The pursuit of a healthy goal that will bring joy may be highly energetic, but it proceeds from a calm and steady inner assurance grounded in being present.

> ➤ For a simple summary of all points thus far, I like to borrow a quotation from Marc Allen. Marc's personal policy is to

always bring his work to fruition *"In an easy and relaxed manner, in a healthy and positive way, in its own perfect time, for the highest good of all."*

➤ *In pursuit of healthy goals that will bring us joy, we seek support. In pursuit of Ego goals, we seek justification and commiseration.* Watch the support groups you become part of, whether formal or informal. A healthy one will be like a healthy A.A. group: people share their "experience, strength and hope." An unhealthy one will be full of people commiserating with one another — "co-miserating," sharing their miseries — and "supporting" one another by justifying their stance as the victim, the noble martyr who bravely presses on, or some such. That's all about the Ego and it's not a support group, it's a drain group.

➤ *Finally, is the motivation primarily intrinsic or extrinsic?* When we do something from intrinsic motivation, we are finding joy and reward in the act itself. With extrinsic motivation, we are doing it to get a reward other than the act itself: the result, the effect, the status and esteem to be gained. Typically, that's Ego.

The last point is tricky. An obvious objection is: what's wrong with results? When we try to do our jobs really well, or perform charity work or try to help our children do well in school, we clearly care about the results, and those results benefit others — don't they?

Of course results matter. It's natural to care about them, and also to think about them. For many activities that are creative or constructive, we *need* to have some vision of the end result in mind, in order to work towards it — and yes, we may "use" that vision as motivation to keep going.

But, but, but. First, let's not confuse "having a plan" with being clear about what you want in life and why it's important to you.

Now, with that distinction in mind, let's consider just a few of the possible pitfalls of being an overly, or exclusively, "results-oriented" person.

Why do you want your kid to do well in school? So that he'll learn, and love to learn? Or so he'll get straight A's and get into Princeton, so that you can be proud of what you've done as a parent instead of feeling guilty that you've blown it? And what does the kid want … ?

For any result you may desire: does the end justify the means? Are you willing to do "whatever it takes" if that requires being destructive or dishonest, or if it compels you to be somebody you aren't?

Perhaps there are many steps to the end result. If you have your eyes on the prize, are you liable to trip over the steps? How careful and creative will you be in carrying them out? Have you heard that people who love the activity itself, and focus on that, are likely to get better results?

If the prize is the only thing, then what do the steps mean to you? Are they just "necessary steps," duties, obstacles along the way? Is there joy in that?

Will you only be happy once you get the result? And what if you don't get the result? Will you then be happy only once you get the next result? If this is the plan, maybe you should keep a score-card. At the end of the roller-coaster ride you'll want to check it to decide whether you can die happy.

Meanwhile you don't need a scorecard to know that you have already qualified for another prize, a tremendous prize, available for claiming right now. You can *live* happy, in the state of joy.

On the Road

Speaking of roller-coaster rides, I would like to close with a story about a wild ride. The story is from my friend Atul:

> Some years ago, Atul and his family were vacationing in Hawaii. They had planned the trip carefully, which included leaving some time open for doing things they might not learn about until they were there. And on the island of Maui, says Atul, "I heard about this place we just had to see. People told me, 'Take the road to Hana. It's really beautiful.'"
>
> Hana, a remote small town along the west coast of Maui, was many miles away. Atul had a large group with him — his own wife and children, his brother-in-law's family, plus

THE STATE OF JOY

another — and by the time he rounded up everyone, it was past noon. They piled into two cars and set off quickly, Atul in the lead.

"We drove like madmen," he says. "The goal was to get to Hana when there was plenty of daylight left, so we could see the sights, do some things and then watch the sunset. We did not intend to stop for food, or anything. We just wanted to get there."

Nice plan, except the road wasn't cooperating. It was a mountainous and winding road above the seashore, full of climbs and dips and hair-raising hairpin turns. With Atul taking it fast, the trip soon started to raise more than hair: "My wife suffers from motion sickness. So do the kids. We had to pull off the road, then pull off again. There were some nice scenic views, and while one person was busy being sick, everybody else would wander off. The kids would be climbing up a big rock or going down some path into the woods. But my brother-in-law is like me, very goal-oriented. As soon as the sick person was feeling better, it was 'Okay, we're all set, let's go!'"

Finally they rolled into Hana, late in the afternoon. What they found left them open-mouthed with astonishment. As Atul puts it, "There was nothing there."

They had arrived at a quiet little town that looked remarkably unremarkable. Some houses, trees, sure — but no eye-catching features, either natural or architectural, nor signs pointing to any. No scenery that compared, even, to what they had briefly glimpsed during their drive. A few shops and restaurants but nothing special and besides, in this tiny town late in the day on a Sunday, "everything was closed." As far as Atul and his people could see, there was "nothing to do, nowhere to go."

Dejected and hungry, they headed back. They missed the sunset by being on a stretch of road that screened the view, then rode the rest of the way in the dark.

Although none of this was amusing at the time, Atul can barely control his laughter when he tells the end of the story. The next day he complained that he had been misled. But in his haste to get going, he had misunderstood: "People said, 'Oh, no! You rushed to Hana? Hana's not the big attraction. It's the *road* to Hana.' That's why they told me to 'Take the road'!"

Many years later Atul learned that visitors come from around the world to travel the road. This explained why he had so often come up behind "slowpokes" who would putter along until they pulled over somewhere, and he learned that these people weren't just enjoying the panorama. They were watching out for the footpaths and side trails that led to the real attractions: the hillsides full of amazing wildflowers. The gorgeous hidden waterfalls, some of them tumbling into crystal-clear pools that one could swim in. The spectacular shoreline below, with cliffs and caves and black sand beaches with the best waves for surfing.

As one guidebook says, "The journey to Hana is not found at the end of the road but along the way." Atul just shakes his head and laughs: "We missed it all!"

The story has become part of the family's folklore, told and remembered often. For anyone like my friend Atul — a good-hearted person who wants the best for himself and others, but who has a tendency to get taken out of being present here and now — the story serves as a reminder of one of the greatest so-called secrets of life. You don't have to "get somewhere" in order to find joy.

One of the many who have made this discovery was the poet T.S. Eliot. Here is how he expressed it, in a poem written late in his life.

> We shall not cease from exploration
> And the end of all our exploring
> Will be to arrive where we started
> And know the place for the first time ...
>
> Quick now, here, now, always —
> A condition of complete simplicity.

You and I, my friend, have now come a long way together since the beginning of this book. The final section that lies ahead is a different kind. It is entirely a collection of brief stories, which are provided for the following purpose.

Although the condition in which we find joy may be, as Mr. Eliot said, one of complete simplicity, our day-to-day lives are not simple. We have lots to do, lots that we want to do, many people in our lives. And, to complicate things, we always carry with us those inner creatures we've learned about. The stories show how they can tangle us up when we're operating in specific settings or Life Spaces ... and each story suggests how *you* can be un-tangled, just by being aware, whenever you face a situation of that type.

I am confident that you will be, for I know what you are. You are the big YOU. And I am confident that you will find profound joy, because after all, it's right here. Where life is, where our not-so-simple and yet wonderfully simple life is. Life is beautiful.

THE STORY BANK

*How our awareness affects us
in the 'Life Spaces' we inhabit*

This final section is a bank of "learning stories" you can draw upon, as you wish, for help in applying the principles outlined in this book.

The core principle that I have emphasized the most is awareness. It is a principle which simply means being present to life, fully and without judgment. We've learned that the joy we derive from living, and the creativity and effectiveness that we are capable of, depend on our level of awareness. Unfortunately, we're not always able to be at the highest level. So what we can learn to do is to be aware of that. If we can recognize when we're functioning at some lower level, it will free us to move upward — and as we learn what being highly aware looks and feels like, it will help us to attain that peak condition more often.

This is where the stories can be useful. They show the typical effects of being at different levels of awareness, in the various aspects of our lives that I call Life Spaces. Whenever you find stories you can relate to, I invite you to take them to heart. Use them as aids in recognizing both the destructive patterns and the healthy patterns in your own life.

Let's quickly review the levels of awareness, then move on to the Life Spaces and the stories.

Three Inner States

Our inner condition is dictated by who's in charge inside. Is it the PIG and the APE? The Ego, coupled with the thinking mind? Or the big YOU? In Chapter 5 we saw that these three basic states correspond to the three levels of awareness, as follows:

Level 1: Unaware — At this level the PIG and APE are running our lives. There are times when they are very helpful, but mostly, they drive us to chase material pleasures and avoid discomfort, and they're also on the lookout to feed and protect the Ego. Not only are we "a slave to our impulses," as some would put it, we are *unaware* of being so.

This is a very limited way to live. The instant pleasures and comforts we get are fleeting, not deeply satisfying. Our actions are purposeful but mostly out of control. We're prone to make rash decisions that cause trouble, and worse, we are blind to the larger possibilities of life.

Level 2: Semi-Aware — Here we use the thinking mind to try to manage our lives. This is usually more fruitful than being Unaware. For example, we may be able to resist instant gratification in favor of some longer-term goal by "adding time" into the equation, and we are generally able to observe the world and make decisions in a logical or rational way.

But this level, too, has its limits. Many life situations can't be handled with pure logic. The quest to mind-manage our inner drives and outer circumstances becomes a constant struggle, if not a losing battle. And the greatest danger at Level 2 is that the mind is not yet decoupled from the Ego.

We may think we're in control but the Ego is directing the show. It puts the mind to work pursuing Ego goals — which in some cases can never be met, and even if they are achieved, do not bring profound joy or harmony. Our best mental efforts can thus be hijacked into the service of an empty, mind-made identity that isn't us at all ... without our being aware of what is happening.

Level 3: Aware — At this level, we have full inner awareness. We can see what our inner creatures are up to. We are no longer blindly under their sway, and we don't need to fight them or manage them, either. Just by being aware of them, we're able to know who we really are.

Now we are living as the big YOU, the core or natural self. Along with our inner awareness, we become exquisitely and joyfully aware of the world around us. We are able to access a larger intelligence in all that we think or do, and rather than trying to control our world, we act in harmony with it.

To learn more about the big YOU, see the video on YouTube titled "Lasting Happiness Starts with Ego Awareness" or visit my website at www.krishnapendyala.com/raising-awareness.

Now, having refreshed our acquaintance with the levels of awareness, let's look at the types of life situations in which we can exercise awareness.

Six Life Spaces

Nearly everything we do occurs within the context of one or more Life Spaces. There are six of these. For an ideal vision, imagine the big YOU as the core of a lotus flower, blossoming out into each of the Life Spaces as follows:

What do these Life Spaces consist of?

Your Self is the space of all activities in your life that are expressly "for you." It includes routine activities like eating and exercising, to nourish your body and keep it in shape, plus activities like planning, reading, taking classes, journaling, or meditating, which you might do for your mental or spiritual self. And yes, it includes all the forms of enjoying or relaxing your self, from using TV and the Internet to taking long hikes in the woods.

The space of *Your Partner* includes everything you think, feel and do in relation to the significant other person in your life: your spouse, boyfriend or girlfriend. If you don't have a partner, it could include thoughts and actions related to a past partner, and/or those involved in finding one.

Your Friends is shorthand for "everyone in your personal life other than your partner and children." It includes your own parents, siblings and relatives — even the ones you aren't on "friendly" terms with — as well as actual friends and acquaintances of all kinds.

Your Work includes all your actions and interactions with respect to what you do to earn a living and contribute to society. If you have means of support other than your work, it would include whatever "occupies" you: attending school, keeping a home, making art, or carrying out projects of any sort.

Your Money is a distinct Life Space in terms of your relationship with it. Once you get money, from work or elsewhere, what do you do with it? Money is a key resource for shaping the circumstances of our lives, so what is your attitude towards it and how do you handle it? This space includes all your motivations for spending, saving, investing and giving.

The last Space, *Your Children,* includes all interactions with your kids. It could also include your relations with other people's children in roles like that of a teacher, youth-group leader or extended family member. If you have no children in your life, you still might want to read the stories in this section: there's plenty here for anyone to enjoy and learn.

The Stories and How to Gain Value from Them

For each Life Space, you'll find stories that describe how people used each of the three levels of awareness to deal with situations within that space. Under "Your Self," for instance, there is a story about a friend of mine who got himself into a bizarre jam by being Unaware, and letting his PIG and APE take charge ... a story about a woman who tried, unsuccessfully, to manage herself by using her mind in service of her Ego ... and the story of a wonderful man I know who has improved himself, over the years, by being highly Aware.

So it goes through the rest of the Life Spaces. There are sure to be some stories that speak to you and you're welcome to pick and choose, referring to a particular one when you find yourself in a similar situation. Indeed the stories have an added feature for that purpose. They all end with "Questions for Learning," which are open-ended questions for you to consider as you go about drawing insights from the stories and applying them to your life.

Final notes: In a few of the stories, people are identified by fictitious first names to protect confidentiality. In three of those —

"Two Weeks and Counting," "Dating: the False Self," and "Better Keep Your Head Down" — various details also are fictionalized, or simplified to make them more generic. Otherwise you're getting everything exactly as I experienced it or as it was related to me, from the experiences of others.

Last but not least, after you've read some stories please be sure to see the closing section, titled Completing and Expanding the Circle. It has just two entries. One is a brief story which, in my view, pulls together lessons from all of the Life Spaces. The other is an invitation to you. I'm asking you to contribute a story of your own, one that can be of value to your fellow readers. Using the book's website, future editions of the book and other means, the goal is to expand the circle of learning and growth begun here.

The story lineup:

LIFE SPACE	LEVEL OF AWARENESS	STORY
YOUR SELF	Level 1	The Incredible Expanding Hamburger
	Level 2	Two Weeks and Counting
	Level 3	Hal — My Hero
YOUR PARTNER	Level 1	The Other Side of Love
	Level 2	Dating: the False Self
	Level 3	A Healthy Union
YOUR FRIENDS	Level 1	Girls' Night Out
	Level 2	The Friendship Triangle
	Level 3	My Guiding 'T' Light

THE INCREDIBLE EXPANDING HAMBURGER

Cutting corners can be risky when they've already been pre-cut. That is one lesson my friend Bill learned during his college days. Like many students, he was a member of ROTC, the U.S. Army's Reserve Officer Training Corps — but not gladly. Bill *hated* ROTC.

He had signed up mainly out of interest in the scholarship money the Army offers. It had seemed like a good deal, since he would also be serving his country. The catch was that military service turned out to disagree with him in every respect. So week after week he went through the motions grudgingly, feeling out of place in the uniform that he had to wear on ROTC days, resenting the drills and routines. Above all he dreaded the field exercises, when Corps members went out into the countryside for entire weekends to live like actual soldiers on maneuvers.

Among the indignities in the field were the portable foods called MREs — which stands for Meals Ready to Eat. These meals were far from gourmet quality and they weren't even ready to eat, just pre-cooked and dehydrated. You had to heat the food with a little heating unit while adding water to re-hydrate it. Then it would swell into chicken stew, noodles with cheese sauce or some other such treat.

On one miserable weekend Bill found himself sitting amid his pile of heavy gear, contemplating an MRE hamburger patty in its pouch. He'd had an MRE burger before. When you re-hydrated the hard little wafer of ground beef it burgeoned into a soggy, sponge-like bundle o' beef. Why bother? Bill was hungry *now,* so he tore open the pouch and ate the patty dry, like a crunchy ground-beef cookie.

Aha! It wasn't bad. He ate another. Then he went back to his duties, deriving a small glow of comfort from his discovery, his small act of rebellion against Army routine.

The glow of comfort did not last. Soon it transformed into terrifying abdominal pain that seemed to be tearing his guts apart. Good heavens, what had he done? Bill was rushed to the nearest E.R. There, after treatment, the doctors told him what had happened. Chunks of the dried burgers had re-hydrated inside his digestive tract. Expanding like the tiny toy animals that grow when you drop them in water, they had sucked up vital fluids and left him severely *de*hydrated internally.

As is often the case in life, a short-cut meant to speed things up nearly brought everything to a halt; instant gratification led to pain later on!

Level 1 Failure

Bill was actually the victim of a conspiracy: his PIG and his APE teaming up to bring him grief. It was the PIG, of course, that literally wanted to be fed right away. But the PIG-ish gobbling of the dried hamburger wasn't just an isolated incident out of the blue. It came out of a background of Bill's long-running resentment of the whole ROTC routine.

Bill's APE had been whining about ROTC constantly: *This is unpleasant; we don't like it; isn't there a way out of this?* And when we fall prey to that kind of APE-chatter inside our heads, it leaves us stuck at a low level of unawareness, unable to be open to much else — such as, in Bill's case, simply accepting that he was in ROTC and being open to what he might learn and gain. What's more, the resentful APE-ish attitude of "I-don't-wanna-be-here-anyway" renders us prone to making rash and rebellious decisions that can backfire. Which is exactly what happened.

Questions for Learning: In your own behavior, do you court trouble via this dangerous PIG-APE combo of corner-cutting grounded in deep resentment of your life situation? Is there a happier and healthier way to face the situation, living as the big YOU?

LIFE SPACE: YOUR SELF / Level 2

TWO WEEKS AND COUNTING

Every springtime in the United States there comes a day of reckoning. For a lot of us it's April 15, income tax day. But here we are talking about May 15.

Recently our young friend Kate (not her real name) had the May 15 blues. Her problem was twofold. In Pennsylvania, swimming pools and beaches open on Memorial Day weekend, which was only two weeks away. Also, she had agreed to be a bridesmaid in a wedding in early June.

So a double deadline had arrived. On the evening of May 15, Kate sat at her computer, nervously searching the Internet. Her search words were "ten pounds in two weeks."

Not many years before, when Kate was in her teens, she had scoffed at the women who went on crash diets to look good in a swimsuit or a bridesmaid's dress. They were slaves to the unrealistic fashion-model image portrayed in the media, she used to say. Why couldn't they learn to accept their own bodies? What fools they were!

Back then, Kate had in fact been about ten pounds overweight. Well, maybe fifteen. Now it was more like twenty-five pounds, maybe close to thirty. Kate, who is good at math, had noticed an ominous trend. She was only gaining about a pound per year, but she was gaining consistently. And at the rate she was going, her number of pounds overweight would always be equal to or greater than her age. Yuk!

That was a troubling thought, the kind that can drive a person to eat. However on May 15 there was still time. Indeed, despite the re-heated slices of pizza that made her fingers greasy as she typed "ten pounds in two weeks" *(look at me: I'm caught red-handed,* she thought, laughing to herself but at the same time disgusted with herself) — despite that, and despite a history of failed diets in the past, there was still time to reverse the trend, just in time for look-good season. And maybe losing ten pounds wouldn't do it but she would at least look more like she used to look, sort of very thoroughly filled out but not so filled up.

Kate's search yielded almost a million hits. She ignored the entries from WebMD and the National Eating Disorders Association, warning against the use of fad diets. What caught her eye was the Cabbage Soup Diet.

With the Cabbage Soup Diet, you could lose ten pounds in *one* week. That would mean a chance to drop twenty pounds in two weeks, or thirty in three. The trick was to eat the soup and nothing but the soup — as much as you wanted, but nothing else. Kate printed out a recipe for this soup. There were a dozen ingredients. Most were not items she kept in her kitchen; she would have to go out and buy them. Then you had to chop the vegetables, and ...

Ironically, Kate never started the soup diet. For a week she carried the recipe in her shoulder bag, yet couldn't face the hassle of buying the stuff and preparing the soup. Was this quick fix not quick enough for her? But when she wasn't busy kicking herself for being so lazy, the glimmer of a deeper insight began to dawn. *Maybe, just maybe, this crash-diet approach wasn't the way to go.* There had to be another way, hadn't there?

Where Level 2 Falls Short

Yes, it is possible to lose weight quickly. Boxers and wrestlers do it to meet the weight limits for their matches. And yes, some people lose weight by eating only a special soup for seven days. The trick is keeping it off, which many people cannot do once the "crash" period is over.

The real trouble is that losing weight becomes an Ego goal. You're doing it solely to look good, often for special occasions when you will be on display. But the pretty picture you'd like to present is just an empty Ego-shell. It doesn't emanate from the core self, the big YOU. All you get is a temporary Ego boost that fades, without the motivation to develop fundamentally healthier habits that could lead to a healthier, happier natural self.

So you backslide until the next special occasion looms ahead. Then the Ego drive kicks in again, and you're off on another crash diet, a vicious cycle.

The PIG and the APE play their parts here, too. Weight gain occurs, in part, because the PIG wants the instant reward of eating what it wants, at any time ... and then, whenever its master the Ego needs to look sharp, the PIG also chases an instant solution for taking off the weight. Meanwhile the APE avoids any fundamental and lasting change: *That sounds like work! Let's stay away from that!* Bottom line: no matter how diligently and rationally your thinking mind may follow the steps of a crash diet — or any other quick-fix solution — you can't make sustained progress if your mind is still coupled to the Ego, pursuing an Ego goal.

Question for Learning: Our friend Kate was left in a hazy in-between state, sensing that there must be "another way" but not sure what it might be. Having read this book, you know that it's the way of the big YOU, building healthy and harmonious habits in keeping with what you really are. What will help you choose that way?

HAL — MY HERO

This story is about a remarkable man who has faced adversity with courage, smarts, and grace, and in the process has ended up enriching the lives of all he comes to know. His name is Hal Williamson, and he is the person to whom I have dedicated this book.

Hal experienced more heartbreak in his early years than many of us will face over a lifetime. At age nine he witnessed his older brother being burned to death in a house fire. On Hal's eleventh birthday, his father was buried after losing a long and nasty battle with cancer.

Although Hal never really excelled in school, each year his teachers — sympathetic to the woes facing his family — would allow him to move on to the next grade. At least until he reached the eighth grade, when the school's principal told his mom they had tested Hal and the results indicated that her son was "retarded." Despite her best efforts to plead Hal's case, the principal said they would not allow her son to graduate and advised her to send him to a trade school.

Hal's mother refused to listen to the principal. She found the money to send Hal to a private school. Despite the extra attention offered there, he didn't do well at first. The turning point came when Hal realized that he needed to work a lot harder than the other kids. He put himself on a rigorous study schedule that required waking up at 3 A.M., then studying after school until he went to bed around 8 P.M. By the end of high school, Hal was in the top of his class.

Things were beginning to look up. Keeping to the same study routine, Hal made further strides in life. He went on to college and earned a degree in mechanical engineering. He worked at the U.S. patent office while studying law at night. Soon he became a patent attorney and worked his way up to the executive suite. But despite these indicators of success, Hal never felt worthy. He actually felt he was cheating the system by secretly working twice as hard as his colleagues. To quiet his thoughts, Hal turned to alcohol.

Luckily, with support from a recovery group, Hal sobered up. His company not only kept him on, but even paid for him to get an MBA. Hal was regarded as more than a patent attorney worth keeping; his employer saw him as a person with great potential. However he did not get to realize that potential with this firm. After a company merger he lost his job entirely.

It would take a long time to find another position comparable to the high-profile one he had held. While searching for employment, Hal made a hobby of researching the brain and how it worked. He wondered if this knowledge could help him understand how he had been able to overcome adversity, and wondered if he could help others with the insight he gained.

Meanwhile, new expenses arose as Hal's children grew up. To help pay their college bills he took a low-level patent attorney job. It was during this time he also developed a seminar on how to use your brain more effectively, called *Pathway to Greatness*. When he introduced it to his colleagues at work, it was met with high acclaim. Before long, people across the country were signing up for his seminars. It seemed he had found a new calling, and life looked brighter than ever. But many more trials lay ahead.

While in Florida to deliver a seminar, Hal and his wife were taking a morning walk when both were struck by a car. Hal's neck and leg were broken. His wife was killed instantly.

After this devastating loss, Hal recovered and dedicated himself to his new mission. He vowed to continue helping people use their brains to enrich the lives of many. After one seminar he met a woman, Sharon Eakes, who could empathize with losing a spouse. Eventually they married — and Sharon, also a psychologist and coach, became Hal's working partner as well. Things were looking up again.

Unfortunately, Hal seemed to be a magnet for disaster. This time it came in the form of a wave of medical problems. Hal broke his hip in a freakish bicycle accident, lost his sight to a rare eye disease, and suffered a stroke. There were so many problems, his doctor referred to him as a "train wreck." Yet Hal did not think of himself in such terms. At the time I write this, he has recovered well from all of these things—even regaining much of his sight through diligent practice of a system he devised for himself, from what he had learned of how the brain works.

And here is perhaps the most amazing thing about Hal. If you were to meet him, given his history of working very hard and rebounding from hardships, you might expect to find him an iron-willed and intensely driven person — a sort of Spartan prototype of stern self-discipline. Hal is indeed well disciplined but that's not how he comes across at all. He radiates happiness and kindness. It is a joy just to be around him, for clearly he loves life.

Every day Hal wakes up excited to write, read, exercise, learn, and share his experience and knowledge with others. That is why, in the dedication to this book, I call him "the happiest man I know"!

My Interpretation

With all the obstacles Hal has faced, he could've easily given up and let his Ego start to believe any of the labels that had been placed on him—retarded child, alcoholic, job-loser, widower, blind and disabled. But he didn't. From early in life, he overcame and achieved success in the public's eye. But obviously something was amiss for a number of years, as even with his early successes, he had to use alcohol to quiet his feelings of inadequacy.

Becoming unemployed and thus getting time to read and discover more about himself might have been the best thing to happen to Hal. Over the course of that time he became enlightened, finding what was really important in his life and what his true mission was. It wasn't to obtain money and prestige. It seemed he'd been going after those things mainly to prove everyone else wrong. He was just letting his PIG and APE reinforce his Ego. As we've learned, that type of motivation can only take one so far, and often in the wrong direction.

Hal has learned to live from the big YOU, from a profound inner happiness. This happiness is the most reliable source of "strength" and "resolve" in the face of difficulties— because if you love life and know that you are a harmonious part of it, as Hal does, then naturally you want to go on engaging with life to the highest of your abilities.

Questions for Learning: When misfortune occurs in your life, what is your initial reaction? With losses such as the death of another, of course there will be grief — but here we're talking about the setbacks that primarily "set back" your own plans, such as things not going the way you wanted them to go at work or in personal life. How do you respond? Is it worthwhile to find the state of being that Hal has found?

THE OTHER SIDE OF LOVE

For nearly three years, Mary and Jake had been going steady. Only high school students, they had met as classmates, and despite their youth they seemed to make a perfect couple. They had fun together, did schoolwork together, and showed affection and consideration to one another. Mary's friends often commented on how lucky she had been to find her soul mate so early on. There was no doubt in her mind that after college or perhaps even during college, she and Jake would wed.

Her fairy tale came to a screeching halt before the end of high school, however. One day, at a time and place she wasn't expecting to see Jake and he apparently wasn't expecting to see her, either, she did see him. With another girl. And not just in that girl's company but obviously, unmistakably "with" her. The shock Mary felt was like the shock of a violent physical accident, which the mind at first cannot even register: *What happened? This can't be!* Then came the pain, and the fury.

Everything hurt, from Jake's betrayal of her trust to the bitter prospect of facing a future without him, because the incident was indeed a relationship-ender. It didn't take long for the pain to coalesce into rage. And Mary's rage channeled itself into a single-minded course of action which, as one of her friends put it, seemed to have a double purpose: getting back at Jake for what he'd done, while reassuring herself of how desirable she was.

Being one of the most beautiful girls in the school, Mary had no problem drawing attention from other guys. A little bit of basic flirting quickly paid off in a steady stream of date requests, free dinners and party invitations. Mary reveled in it all, and above all she seemed to want certain people to know about her romantic escapades and the names of her latest suitors. If you watched closely, you'd have noticed that she was carrying out her adventures very visibly, and talking about them very freely, in front of the people who would be most likely to pass the news along to Jake.

Dating for Mary started to resemble a competitive sport, in which the points didn't count unless Jake knew about them. The more guys she could get to fawn over her, thus demonstrating her value, the more Jake would realize what a mistake it had been to dump her.

One might think the game would have wound down when Mary went off to college. Time was passing and the setting was different — Jake was no longer nearby, nor were there many members of the old high-school gang on this campus to keep Jake informed of her doings. However, the game got worse. By now Mary had seen the power she was able to exert over men, and acted almost as if she was addicted to it.

She went on having flings with one guy after another. The encounters grew more serious, in many cases, than the superficial dates she'd had in high school. Yet none developed into a lasting relationship and she was constantly moving on to the next one. It would be a long while before Mary could build the kind of life she had once envisioned — with a relationship that's grounded in caring and brings not discontent, but deep happiness.

A Self-Defeating Reaction

At some point, you may have been dumped by someone you thought you were destined to be with, as Mary was. It is natural to feel heartbreak and it may well take some time to get over it. Notice, however, that Mary didn't take much time at all to mourn or heal or reflect. She swung into counter-action almost immediately, chasing rapid-fire romances that delivered quick gratification without deep satisfaction, then proceeded to dig herself deeper into that rut for years and years.

Her love life had been hijacked by her inner creatures. And while it may seem that the PIG was the main culprit, I would suggest that Mary's trouble began with her APE. The process of dealing with being dumped — really facing up to it, and reflecting upon one's own feelings as well as upon "what happened" — strikes the APE as a difficult and painful experience in itself. The APE wants to avoid that by all means: *My master, the Ego, has been wounded enough!*, it says. *We can't prolong the pain by dwelling on it!*

From there, Mary's PIG was more than ready to play its part. Off it took her, on that multi-year chase of other guys — chasing distraction from the pain, chasing vengeance on Jake, chasing instant rewards and Ego gratification. And also chasing the ultimate Ego goal, which was to make Jake so jealous that he'd suddenly show up at her door begging "Oh, I was wrong to hurt you, take me back, please!"

Which brings us to the punch line. The wish came true. One day Mary had a visitor, and the visitor was Jake. This was the day she had long been waiting for, and she did what she had been longing to do. She threw him out. There's an old saying, "Revenge is a dish that tastes best cold." That may be so, but one has to wonder, how satisfying is it? Doesn't it also just taste ... cold?

Questions for Learning: It's almost inevitable that each of us will at some time be hurt deeply, if not dumped, by someone we care about. So what is the healthy way to respond? You don't want to take Mary's path but you don't want to wallow endlessly in grief and isolation, either. That's the inner creatures hijacking your love life in another way: feeding and protecting your Ego's identity as the unjustly wounded victim. Isn't there a healthier alternative — one that starts from inner awareness?

LIFE SPACE: YOUR PARTNER / Level 2

DATING: THE FALSE SELF

"It's more than wanting to make a 'good impression,'" Jason said, forming a set of air-quotes with his fingers. "If you really like a woman you've just met, you want to be the kind of person that you think *she* would like."

Jason, now middle-aged, was recently separated from his wife. He was sharing his story to help me understand how the blind date of his dreams could have led to a marriage that turned out so badly. After all, the courtship had been passionate and every date was truly an adventure. Or so it had seemed at the time.

She wanted to stay in and have a quiet evening on Saturday night? That wasn't his style ... but what the heck, he had partied enough in his lifetime; he might as well try this for a change. And her friends? Frankly, he had never cared much for hanging out with PhD students or university professors. But he did like to show off his intellectual side once in a while, and these people laughed at the witty remarks he put in whenever they would let him.

What Jason had been doing, in these ways and others, went beyond the adjustments that one always has to make in relating to a partner. He was playing a role — "pretending to be who I wasn't," he now says. He would later learn, to his great dismay, that in many cases his dream girl was doing it too. "Hey, we were infatuated. It makes you do stupid things," he explains. Moreover, "neither of us was getting younger. Everybody around us was married and I think we were both in a little bit of a rush to get locked in, find a mate."

The courtship period was brief, with just a few months from first date to wedding day. Jason reflected that "maybe subconsciously, we knew we had to move fast. Faster than the speed of disillusionment."

It wasn't long before the shell of pretense wore thin and broke. Jason was shocked, for instance, to find that his dream girl no longer shared his love of roughing it in the great outdoors. Their camping trips became bad trips as she complained constantly about minor problems like mud and mosquitoes. For him, the quiet nights at home were a bore, exceeded only by the nights when her colossally boring friends came to dinner. His witty remarks to them were growing more like insults, and when his wife started glaring he'd excuse himself to make a very important phone call.

Clashes in underlying values began to surface. Every decision — whether it was about spending money or spending the holidays with family members — seemed to set off an argument, until at last a separation seemed the only answer.

Such differences! How had they gone unnoticed?

The Ego Trap

Jason and his dream girl fell into a trap that catches many of us. It's the trap of putting on an act, a false front, in order to get what you think you want or need. This happens very frequently in dating and the result is often the same. Two people get married who've never really met.

That is, their core or natural selves have never met, because for both of them the big YOU was obscured by the Ego, or just by the PIG in lust. When it comes to dating, the Ego isn't truly very interested in the other person. The Ego wants, and feels that it deserves, "a relationship" — a sort of object that is quite different from the healthy human process of actually relating. Therefore, when someone comes along who seems suitable for providing that object, the PIG leaps forward in service of its master and says: *Bingo! Let's have it. We're in love!*

Then comes the insidious part. The thinking mind, in thrall to the Ego, papers over the differences. The mind also cooks up justifications for putting on a false act to lure in the other person. As Jason noted, "I can see that I was play-acting, but it didn't feel like it back then. One benefit of meeting somebody new is the chance to get into that person's world — to expand your horizons, you know? So I convinced myself that I wasn't really 'pretending' to like what she liked, even when my friends made comments to that effect. I told them I was opening up to new influences, becoming a better and more well-rounded guy."

Jason, of course, was merely repeating to his friends the story that his Egoic mind had made up, in order to rationalize the whole affair. Small wonder it became a doomed affair.

Questions for learning: When you find yourself caught up with pursuing a new goal in life, whose goal is it? If you are willing to distort who you really are to get the goal, is that perhaps a warning sign that it's an Ego goal?

LIFE SPACE: YOUR PARTNER / Level 3

A HEALTHY UNION

If you have ever started a business from the ground up, you know the trials, tribulations, and tight cash flow that characterize such a time. It is hard enough for someone single, but imagine going through this period as part of a couple with three young children to support. Vasco Pedro and his wife Maria have not only been doing it, they've been doing it joyfully, as one of the happiest couples I am privileged to know.

Originally from Portugal, Vasco and Maria came to the U.S. in 2001 so Vasco could pursue a master's degree at Carnegie Mellon University here in Pittsburgh. They planned to stay only a couple of years, which got extended when Vasco decided to go on and earn a PhD in computer science. For a while during his student days the couple got by on moderate financial terms. There were only the two of them, and Vasco's program of study paid him a stipend while Maria worked as a librarian.

Maria, however, was eager to step away from her career to begin having and raising children. This was a dream she had cherished. It is also a dream that can cause tremendous tension and friction for young couples in such a situation. The graduate-student husband is liable to argue: "We can't have children now! Wait till I finish school and get a good job!" The woman may accept this argument but then resent the notion that her husband's goals have to come before hers, or worry that the long-awaited tomorrow will never come.

Maria and Vasco didn't get caught in that emotional trap. They had a built a marriage with a synergistic spirit, a spirit that says: *We can pursue our goals and dreams together. Although it may not be easy, we will be happy and make each other happy, so let's do it.*

While Vasco was earning his PhD, Maria left her job and gave birth to two gorgeous little girls. Their two-bedroom apartment became rather cramped, and they couldn't afford a larger one — or, for that matter, any of the amenities that many of us take for granted — since Vasco's stipend from the university was now their only source of earned income. So they had a squeezed situation, but one brimming with shared joy. It also wasn't long before Vasco would receive his degree and be able to find a well-paying position somewhere.

You may think, "Well, that doesn't sound so tough. A lot of poor families have a much harder road." But keep in mind that Maria and Vasco were living in a setting where expectations are higher than they are for the least fortunate of us, and people in any stratum of society can get frustrated when expectations aren't met. Consider, too, what happened next.

Vasco was presented with a path other than that well-paying job on the horizon. He had an opportunity to launch a startup company based on his doctoral research. That would mean not only much less income than the couple had hoped for, but a huge amount of work as an early-stage entrepreneur. This is where the tensions and the frictions can really escalate.

It wouldn't have been surprising at all for Maria to put her foot down, taking a stand like: *You can't do this, Vasco! We have to think of the children; you have to think of me; you have to get a job and the startup will have to wait!* It would also be common for someone in Vasco's position to fire back with: *I can't pass up a chance like this! What you have to do, Maria, is help carry us through. Get a job yourself; put the kids in day care, and whatever we do let's not have any more kids!*

Again, though, this couple chose the high road, despite knowing that it would be the difficult road. Maria put herself heartily behind Vasco's dream of starting a company. And with Vasco on board emotionally for his part, neither did she have to defer her own dream of having another child. As it happened, the joint dreams could not have coincided more nicely. On the very day that Vasco's new company, a firm called Bueda, was formally incorporated, Maria delivered their third daughter, Sofia.

What It Takes

Vasco is someone I've had the good fortune to know personally. I find him to be an extremely pleasant young man, full of gratitude, with a zest for life and a glimmer of hope in his eyes. Although I don't know Maria personally I have often heard stories about the unconditional love and support she gives to Vasco, and her creative budgeting which makes the household work. People who meet the couple see very few signs of the stresses that consume many young families living under financial and material constraints, and when they meet the daughters they see happy children being raised lovingly.

What does it take to have such a life together? I would point to two things. One is simply knowing what's important in life. Yes, there are times we're all going to worry about money — but why do so many of us think we need so much of it? Do we really think we'll find joy in expensive designer clothes, or in 5,000-square-foot houses that may just distance our children from us, or in luxury cars that we'll spend every waking moment worrying about someone scratching? Of course not. Maria and Vasco have had none of these things and they are happier than most people I've met who have it all. Profound joy comes from doing what we are called to do. And from supporting our partners in what they are called to do.

The other thing it takes is one you've probably guessed: each partner living as the big YOU, not run by their inner creatures. In a home like Vasco and Maria's, cramped and yet thriving, there is no room for PIGs and APEs running wild through the tiny apartment. Nor, in a life lived so closely together in every respect, is there room for Egos to stake out their separate territories. The common ground created by a union of two big YOUs is far more wonderful. Each person is fulfilled as an individual, and together they have a joy that neither would find alone.

Questions for Learning: While the circumstances of your life situation may not be the same as Maria and Vasco's, are there insights here that you could apply? And can YOU, meaning your very own big YOU, take the initiative in applying them — rather than wishing your partner would get better? Isn't that where it begins?

LIFE SPACE: YOUR FRIENDS / Level 1

GIRLS' NIGHT OUT

Here's a story sent to me by a young woman I work with:

"My friends and I would occasionally plan a girls' night out on the weekends.

We all would get ready together, have a few drinks, and then head out to the local bars. On paper it seems like a great way to catch up with your girlfriends and blow off some steam. However, these occasions always seemed to have another implicit element built in: a fierce competition among friends, which was only amplified with alcohol.

"Going into these nights, everyone knew there would be 'prizes' awarded. Not real trophies but just a consensus on who 'won' for the best outfit, best shoes, best makeup, best hair; or who was the skinniest, the most photogenic—because of course there would be a camera to document the night's events—with the awards determined by which girl got the most attention at the bar, or got the most comments on Facebook the morning after. It would take forever to get ready because the girls would constantly change their outfits to ensure that they weren't out-dressed: 'Oh, you're wearing a dress tonight? Hold on...I'll—I'll be right back.' And when the attention came from men at the bars, the girls would always pretend that they didn't want guys to check them out or talk to them. But it was quite clear that none of us were dressing this way, in uncomfortable heels and skin-tight pants, for each other or for ourselves.

"Even women in serious relationships played these games. I had a roommate who would occasionally go out without her boyfriend of two years. She would flirt with other men — sometimes stealing them from talking with our other single friends — to get drinks and flattery. It wasn't until they asked for her number that she would giggle and say, 'Oh, I'm already taken.' Sometimes she would even agree to a date or give men her number and then never answer their calls, complaining to me and my other roommate about how annoying it was.

"I believe that many women playing these games are unaware of what they're doing and how it's affecting their friendships and relationships. They insist they are just dressing up to suit their own taste and really are not interested in the men in the bars, and this may very well be what their Ego is telling them. Hopefully, one day they will realize that maybe this isn't really what they want, and that what's going on is more like their PIGs feeding their Egos."

An Additional Animal

My young colleague has read the situation well. I would point out that the APE is probably a factor here, too. For instance there appears to be a focus on taking men's attention away from the other girls — not out of genuine interest in a particular guy, but just to show that you can hook him and the competition can't.

Getting outdone by the other girls would be a blow to the Ego, a painful experience that it is the APE's job to avoid.

Questions for Learning: To a degree, it can be natural and healthy for friends to compete at things. But in cases like this one — where the competition is at the crudest level of PIG-APE-Ego dynamics, and it becomes a focal point of getting together, despite a lot of pretense and denial that this is so — has the "game" gotten out of proportion? Does it crowd out the real opportunity for friends to grow closer and build up one another? Are there situations in your life where you are unknowingly letting this happen?

LIFE SPACE: YOUR FRIENDS / Level 2

THE FRIENDSHIP TRIANGLE

In middle school, Rhonda and LeAnn were inseparable. Rhonda would sleep over at LeAnn's house every Friday night, and on Saturday nights the girls would switch homes. It was evident in school that the girls had a special connection and friendship of the kind that you usually only read about in novels.

A girl named Marcy, who shared some classes with each of them, observed this and felt a bit jealous. Driven by a yearning to be part of the girls' special bond, and eager to join those sleepovers that sounded like so much fun, she came up with a cunning plan she thought would get her in with Rhonda and LeAnn.

To curry favor with Rhonda, Marcy casually made an unflattering remark to her — and when Rhonda took offense, Marcy acted surprised and said she was just repeating something that LeAnn had said. Likewise, to earn LeAnn's trust, Marcy made up yet another fictitious negative comment, shared it with her and attributed it to Rhonda. Marcy's strategy was to pry the friends apart just a little while making room for herself, thus turning the twosome into a friendship triangle.

Her plan, however, did not play out as she had expected. The two friends were extremely hurt by the comments. Their mutual trust was deeply shaken. At a more mature stage of life, they might have absorbed this blow and talked the incidents over with each other, thereby figuring out what Marcy was up to. But they wouldn't learn of Marcy's role until later, too late. Instead, they fell so hard for the trick that their bond was poisoned and they began to drift apart ... leaving Marcy stranded in the widening gulf between them.

So not only did Marcy fail to create her triangle, she had also caused the magical friendship between LeAnn and Rhonda to deteriorate. By the time the two girls left for college, they barely spoke. Many years afterward, when LeAnn and Marcy met as adults, LeAnn still recalled what Marcy had done to her and Rhonda.

How Our Egos Get the Best of Us
By Bringing Out the Worst in Us

When two friends have a very close bond, it's natural for those around them to feel somewhat excluded. Still, it is quite possible to work one's way into the friendship — becoming a sort of "next-best friend" of the pair, if not a co-equal — by being good-natured and sincere and contributing to the enjoyment all around.

This cannot be done if one's Ego is in charge, however. And Marcy's story shows that the Ego can take control at an early age, well before adulthood. Marcy's Ego wasn't willing to accept any next-best status, even temporarily. Her PIG, the Ego's servant, insisted that *master is entitled to full membership!*, and drove her to go for that goal by the quickest manner that her thinking mind could think of.

How do we know if this is a correct analysis of what went on inside a young teenager's head long ago? While there is no way of being certain, certain telltale pieces of evidence point to it. For one thing, the plan Marcy came up with was a cruel one, showing no consideration for Rhonda's or LeAnn's feelings — and that's a hallmark of the Ego. The Ego is concerned only with itself, even in matters such as making friends.

Furthermore, both her plan and her goal were pretty unrealistic: getting on equal terms with two longtime best friends by slandering each one to the other? Put in those plain terms, it sounds delusional, which indeed it was. And as we've learned in this book, that is another sign of the Ego: being a mind-made delusion, it leads us to act delusionally.

Finally, while middle-schoolers may be inexperienced, they are not stupid. Despite acting from her Ego, a girl with a clever and calculating mind like Marcy's could have seen that her tactics were ill-fated just by looking ahead a little and thinking through the angles, but someone being pulled by the PIG doesn't have that ability to look ahead. As we've seen repeatedly, the inner animals, the PIG and the APE, are "blind instincts." Marcy wasn't just Ego-deluded, she was flying blind, and that's how friendships are wrecked.

Questions for Learning: Unhealthy patterns we acquire in our early years can persist all through life unless we become aware of them. Do you recognize any of Marcy's tendencies in your own interactions with friends?

Also, here's another way to learn from this story. Marcy set out to "win" friends by making other people lose, and as we saw in Chapter 8, win-lose is a classic Ego strategy that *always degenerates to lose-lose* — everybody loses, as happened in this case. Do you ever play win-lose with friends and acquaintances? How could you transform that to win-win?

MY GUIDING 'T' LIGHT

Dr. T, Jim Thompson, was my advisor in graduate school. I met him a few years after a sudden heart attack almost cost him his life. Since then, his whole attitude towards life has been one of gratefulness. Each day he wakes up appreciative of what he's been able to experience and participate in.

Although he was the chair of his academic department, Dr. T was never intimidating. Even the lowliest undergraduates were comfortable approaching him with issues, in part because of his great sense of humor. There's a story he told on himself which still makes me laugh to this day, and helps illustrate the nature of the man: Driving to Michigan one day, Dr. T let himself go a bit too fast. He was pulled over for speeding. When the cop asked him the typical question — "What's the hurry?" — he replied with a straight face, "I am taking my mother-in-law back home." The cop smiled and said, "Good luck with that, just take it a little easy."

Dr. T's mother-in-law was in fact right there in the car with him, and naturally he couldn't have dared to make such a crack unless he had a strong relationship with her. Which he did, and which enabled him to do what he has so often done: lighten up a touchy encounter by turning it into a laugh for everyone.

He is a great friend to all he meets and a well-wisher, always looking out for the interests of others. Moreover, while we often say of kind-hearted people that they can "see the good in everyone," Dr. T goes further. He can see the *best* in everyone. He had hopes and dreams for the students he advised that went beyond what they could imagine for themselves.

Having been one of those students, I can also attest that he wasn't merely the kind of starry-eyed optimist who makes you shake your head and think *yeah, yeah, that'll never happen*. He recognized potential in us that we had yet to recognize, and he helped us to see it, and inspired us to fulfill it.

We could learn from him, too, how to handle adversity. Once, Dr. T was involved in a business deal that went south in a way that would make most people extremely upset and angry. His response was one of reflection: "I should have been more careful."

Postscript

Dr. T has remained an important person in my life through the more than two decades that have passed since my school days. I still talk to him every couple of months and see him once or twice a year. In addition to being a loving father of his own two children and four grandchildren, he has played the role of my adopted U.S. father and grandpa to my children, and his wife Jeanette is my daughter's godmother.

Does this man have flaws? Well, surely he does — but in terms of how he relates to others, I can think of only one possible beef. Dr T. is so selfless in his unconditional devotion to his students, friends and family that he never accepts any credit when I try to tell him how much he has meant to me. Whenever I talk about the formative impact he's had on my life, he'll always respond with a modest, "Oh, I didn't do much."

That couldn't be further from the truth. Dr. T, as my advisor, then my friend, and my role model for many years, gave me the confidence and courage to pursue anything I wanted.

Questions for Learning: There is so much depth and breadth in the qualities of Dr. T's friendship that I am not sure what questions to pose to you, other than asking if you have noticed the absence of Ego in what you've read about him. I've mentioned only a few of the things that I have been able to learn from him, and to quote Michelangelo's motto, "I am still learning." So here is the best question. Can you find a friend and mentor like Dr. T in your life — someone you can keep learning from, who can be your guiding light?

LIFE SPACE: YOUR WORK / Level 1

'NO ONE WILL EVER KNOW'

Even in slow economic times, hundreds of thousands of new homes are built in the U.S. every year. Clearly home-building is a big industry, and for the customers, buying a home is a big deal. It's the biggest single expense that many people incur and the most important physical asset they will own.

Sadly, according to figures from the Better Business Bureau, about 10% of new-home buyers are dismayed to find that their homes haven't been built properly. Although any construction project is bound to have imperfections, here we are talking about flaws that could lead to major repairs or worse. Further investigation often shows that the builders cut corners, either by rushing their work or by leaving out critical steps.

Some of the more serious problems can take root in the early stages of construction: choosing the site, excavating and preparing the soil, pouring the foundation. All new homes "settle" to a degree, over time. If the early work isn't done with due care, or if it is rushed in ways like not giving the concrete enough time to cure, a home can settle and shift severely, springing cracks and leaks, twisting doorways out of shape and generally raising havoc. Yet nothing may appear to be wrong when the buyer first moves in, making these flaws hard to detect as well as hard to correct.

Other problems range from support beams put in wrong to missing hurricane clips on roof truss connections — imagine your roof lifting away — and poor brick and masonry work. Among the worst cases was one reported by Elizabeth Leamy of ABC News in November 2006 on *Good Morning America:*

> One Maryland house had drastic structural problems. The contractor shoved the main support beam through the outside wall when he couldn't get it to fit right on the other end.
>
> Inside the house, inspector J.D. Grewell said the entire roof could come crashing down because it was installed wrong. "This is to the point of let's start over, let's start rebuilding," he said.
>
> Fortunately, the homeowners discovered these life-threatening flaws before the drywall went up and hid them from view. "It has been a total nightmare," said Dennis Capolongo, owner of the Maryland home. "We are devastated. It has taken away lots of precious time from my family and friends."

Sometimes, especially during building booms, problems like these have been traced to over-extended builders hiring inexperienced workers and pressing them into action. In other cases, companies have had skilled crews and supervisors who surely knew the right way to do things, yet it seemed that somebody, somewhere along the line, decided to take shortcuts in order to meet deadlines or financial goals — or just to reduce the work they had to do.

'Faster, Cheaper, Better' vs. 'Faster, Cheaper, Worse'

Cutting corners is different from making mistakes, which can happen even when we're trying to do our best. In corner-cutting, we know what ought to be done and choose not to do it. We skip certain steps in the process or do them halfway, or we short-change the job in other respects.

Corner-cutting is also different from finding ways to work more efficiently. When we strive for efficiency we set out to do the work "faster, cheaper, and better," meaning better for all concerned, a win-win all around. When we cut corners we are typically out to make it faster or cheaper for ourselves — and we're willing to let the results be worse for somebody else. We figure "no one will ever know" because the shortcomings aren't noticeable right away, but they are liable to produce unpleasant surprises later on.

People in every line of work are apt to cut corners, not just home-builders. It's a type of behavior that is hard for many of us to resist, as it comes from the PIG and the APE ganging up together. The PIG is greedy for the rewards at the end, such as the money or the free time once the job is finished. The APE wants to avoid the extra work required to get things right, and it may also want to avoid other painful experiences, like having to admit that the job isn't on schedule. Each drives us to ignore the standards for the kind of work we are doing. Neither cares about the long-term consequences. That's why the PIG-APE combo is a dangerous pair.

The combo can even be fatally dangerous: we often hear in the news about tragic accidents that occurred after companies or workers ignored safety standards. And in countless more cases, cutting corners simply turns out to be a lose-lose proposition that affects the corner-cutters along with those who rely on their work. A person or company gets away with substandard work until the customers decide they're not going to put up with it, or a public official or a news reporter discovers what's going on.

It's foolish to think that no one will ever know. Only someone who is being run by his PIG and APE — and doesn't even know it — would think that way.

Questions for Learning: Have you ever cut corners in your work, and if so, what drove you to do it? Is this a choice that produces a win-win? Or could somebody, including yourself, lose and be harmed? And here's a tough one: If cutting corners is "business as usual" in your workplace, something that everybody is expected to do, then what is the healthiest response you can make?

LIFE SPACE: YOUR WORK / Level 2

'BETTER KEEP YOUR HEAD DOWN'

John had been at his new job for almost a year. It hadn't been easy, but after struggling to learn the ropes and fit in, he had contributed a great idea — a plan for a faster way of filling customer-service orders. The company was now using the plan, which saved money while making the customers happier, too.

This was a time for John to be feeling deeply satisfied. Instead, he was angry. It turned out that his boss, Seth, had passed the idea along to upper management without giving John any credit.

In addition to being angry, John was mystified. He remembered going to Seth's office to explain the idea. He remembered Seth praising his work and thanking him for a job well done. Then somehow the story changed. By the time the plan took effect, everyone from the company president on down was talking about it as Seth's plan for improving service.

John's head was abuzz with resentful speculation. Had Seth simply "stolen" the idea, presenting it as his own to get recognition from the higher-ups? Or had the higher-ups misunderstood whose idea it was — but if so, why didn't Seth set the record straight? And was it just John's imagination, or was Seth avoiding him in the hallways lately?

There was only one thing to do. John needed to make another visit to Seth's office, to have a frank conversation about the whole matter. Unfortunately, John never took that step. Rather than trying to clear the air, he listened to the nattering of his co-workers. "Better keep your head down," they'd tell him. "Confronting your department head will make it worse." Or: "This place is a snake pit. Too many people out for themselves, and you can't trust anybody. Unless you want to get chewed up, you've just got to watch your back and lay low."

The co-workers saying these things were the ones who had struck John as being negative and unproductive people when he first joined the company. Yet now they seemed like allies: they felt his pain, they commiserated with him! And John fell in line with their advice.

Communicating with Seth was now out of the question. So was the notion of coming up with any more brilliant ideas in the future. From this point, John would do only what his job required and no more. That would protect him from being hurt again and leave him plenty of time to do what others in his department liked to do: sit around and complain.

Analysis of the Breakdown

This is a classic example of PIG-APE-Ego behavior poisoning a workplace. The PIG behavior came from the department head, Seth, when he somehow "appropriated" John's idea for his own gain and to feed his Ego. John, for his part, let himself be led by his APE when he avoided the necessary but perhaps painful step of having a face-to-face with Seth. And the worst part about such behavior is that it can become self-reinforcing.

Seth and others are encouraged to act like PIGs if they know they won't be called out. This in turn confirms the fears of the APEs in the department, who respond by huddling together and muttering about the fact that it's a jungle out there. Misery loves company, and after a while, nobody who's well-balanced wants to work there. Trust and communication are shut down; innovation is stifled.

Questions for Learning: Does anything like this happen in your work? Can you be the big YOU who breaks the pattern?

LIFE SPACE: YOUR WORK / Level 3

FROM LOSE-LOSE TO WIN-WIN

Back in 1995 my multimedia training company, Visual Symphony, ran into a situation that needed some legal help to sort out a misunderstanding.

We had just finished a custom training project for a large corporation. Their management team had the impression that by paying for the project, the corporation owned not only the training program, but also the computer software and other items we had developed to deliver the type of training their staff had received. My company did not see it this way. Independently, we had invested two years of work plus our own resources to build up the software platform. It was meant to be used for many clients, on various projects. I knew we would have to bring in attorneys, but at that point my company did not have the money for such legal expenses.

Luckily Tom Levine, our advisor, gave some advice that helped immensely. Since then I have been able to use his wisdom whenever it comes to negotiating in business or in other areas of my life.

After years of practicing law, Tom had left the field. He had discovered, the hard way, that many of the incentives for advancing one's career in a law firm point in the wrong direction. For instance, he told me, attorneys who solve a client's problem quickly cannot count on winning praise from their superiors. If you want to earn bonuses and be made a partner at a law firm, you have to generate revenue for the firm. The way to do that is by billing lots of hours.

With his past experience in mind, Tom advised me to try and work out an agreement with the other party before the lawyers got involved. We should only bring them into the mix to draft the language in the agreement, he said. This would cut the time it took to get the deal done and reduce our financial burden, a smart plan, since we couldn't possibly afford to hang in with the other side in any sort of protracted legal battle. Most important, he advised me: "Always walk into a business negotiation thinking about the other parties' vested interest and propose a solution to address it."

Tom was then able to set me up with Carl, an attorney he respected. I met with Carl and told him about both parties' vested interests. My client, the large corporation, mainly had an interest in protecting the content of its custom training, to keep it from reaching competitors or any others who might profit from it. My company's interest was retaining the ability to use the software "shell" for other clients. I also mentioned that I was on an extremely tight budget, and asked Carl to seek my permission for doing any further work when the bill went over $500 — which is chump change for high-priced attorneys.

Although Carl thought I was crazy at the time, and told me that no one had ever requested his permission for charging more than $500, I am happy to report that Tom's strategy worked. We resolved the matter to both companies' satisfaction and our legal bill was a mere $750, much lower than the thousands it would normally cost.

The Usual Way vs. Tom's Way

Typically in a negotiation, the opposing parties are truly "opposed." They come to the table thinking only about themselves. They have been advised to be fully mindful of the other party's viewpoint and wants, but only in terms of how this affects their own objectives. They are told to think carefully about their walk-away positions before getting emotionally involved, and to keep looking over the list of things they want.

With this mindset, the parties can go no higher than the Level 2 decision-making we discussed in Chapter 7. The people on each side *think* they're in control of the situation, because they've got a logical game plan. Their wishes may be valid but the wish lists are usually held as Ego goals, with everybody's PIGs primed to go after the items on the lists.

What ensues? The two sides will fight for what they want until a compromise is reached, and compromising is the ultimate Ego trap. While the Egos on each side can think that they "won" — which they will try to do, by coming up with a story that says "we got as much as we could" — the only way to reach a compromise is by giving up things in return. Thus in fact, each side has had to lose something and therefore, usually neither side is truly happy. Meanwhile a lot of time and often much money has been spent to reach the outcome, creating further losses for all concerned.

Tom's advice, developed after years of observing first-hand the convoluted and stressful process of business negotiations, is wise. His words help us see that perhaps lose-lose situations like this can be turned into win-win situations, where both parties understand each other and leave the table happier than when they came.

Questions for Learning: How do you negotiate? Could Tom's advice — "Always walk into a business negotiation thinking about the other parties' vested interest and propose a solution to address it" — be applied to situations in your work life? And in your personal life as well?

LIFE SPACE: YOUR MONEY / Level 1

AHEAD OR BEHIND?

A friend who travels a lot on business tells me that some of his best, and strangest, insights into human nature come from random encounters with people along the way. There was the time he was riding in a cab when the driver started to boast about his winnings in the state lottery. "Last year alone I hit it big three times," the young man said. "Once for about a thousand bucks, once about six hundred and once about five hundred."

My friend asked him what he spent on lottery tickets over the course of a year. The driver said, "I play ten dollars a day." After quickly doing the mental math, my friend decided it was best to say nothing. All was silent until the cab driver called out, "So, um, how much does that put me ahead?"

Let's get in touch with the realities that the driver seemed to miss. Lotteries are designed to make a profit. They pay out much less than they take in, overall. This means that by betting frequently over a long period, you may increase your chances of getting "winning tickets" once in a while, but your chances of coming out ahead *dollar-wise* are very, very small. The odds are stacked against you. Since most state lotteries pay back around 60% of the money wagered, your average for the long run will probably be close to that. You'll get back somewhat more than half of the money you put in — and lose the rest.

Which is what happened to our driver. If he "won" a total of $2100 by betting $10 per day over a year, or $3650, he had a net loss of $1550.

Stuck in the PIG and APE Pattern

Clearly the cab driver would do better just to put his money into a savings account. There would be no losses, and at the end of each year he'd have a full $3650, plus some interest, to spend as he saw fit.

But why doesn't he do it? Why don't the legions of chronic lottery losers across the country do it? How could they be so oblivious to the drain on their resources; what makes them persist in a fast-money PIG behavior that has so little chance of paying off?

Some are addicted and need help. As for the rest, the cab driver can offer a couple of clues to how people rationalize this basic irrationality. Notice that he didn't speak of his bets as "spending." His words were, "I *play* ten dollars a day." There's a certain pride in the statement. It says you are literally a "player," someone willing to go for a big score — which is a more glamorous identity for the Ego than that of a sensible squirrel putting away nuts for the future.

This may also help explain why the driver didn't even keep track of losses versus winnings. That kind of petty reckoning is for squirrels. It doesn't fit with the identity. Besides, adding up the totals to discover that you are behind would threaten the Ego drastically. The APE says: *Don't worry. Keep playing.* The whole game is a giant PIG-and-APE fantasy, in which the Ego-driven gambler only cares to recall the many glorious days when he played, and the still more glorious days when he won.

Questions for Learning: Are there areas of your financial life in which you don't keep track of the money? Is it possible that a lot more is flowing out than you might suspect? Could your PIG, APE and Ego be conspiring to keep you from getting a handle on things?

LIFE SPACE: YOUR MONEY / Level 2

KEEPING UP WITH THE JONESES

I often pose this question to people I'm coaching: "If you owned a fabric store, would you allow customers to bring in their own yardsticks to measure the fabric they buy from you?" Almost everyone responds with a "No" and something along the lines of, "It's my store and I'd use my own standard of measurement." I then inquire, "Then why do you allow your life to be measured by other people's standards?"

The extent to which many of us do this is truly amazing. We become so obsessed with "measuring up" to others that we focus on acquiring the outward signs of success and achievement, rather than inner happiness. We even worry about how we are judged by strangers we'll never see again, which is like letting random passersby, who will never set foot in your store, dictate how you're going to operate it!

This practice of measuring ourselves against neighbors, peers, or colleagues almost seems to be ingrained in our American culture and many others as well. In an effort to keep up with the fictitious Joneses, we find ourselves doing things like embellishing our accomplishments, getting into expensive pastimes not because they're so enjoyable but because they're so fashionable, and building additions to our homes just to show that we're doing as well as the people in the bigger houses down the road.

But worst of all is when we begin to finance such lifestyles with debt. Lifestyles that, if we were to reflect upon them, we probably don't really want.

A Citibank marketing campaign some years ago promoted the slogan "Live Richly," showing people how they could have anything they wanted and pay for it on credit. The invitation on one billboard read: "Open a cravings account."

In my own city, many years ago, there was a fund-raising campaign to build a place of worship. I was told that it soon became a competition as to who would show up higher on the list of donors on the plaque at the entrance of the new temple. In this instance, the end result was more funds to build a big temple, which seems to be a worthy outcome. However the motivation was to keep up with or beat the Joneses. We have all seen such motivations in many different areas of our lives.

What Are You Getting for Your Money?

"Keeping up with the Joneses" behavior is essentially an Ego game. The part of ourselves we're trying to cultivate and build up is the identity that we present to others, which is the Ego. This is not a very satisfying game to begin with, and if we start borrowing beyond our means to keep up the identity it can become downright self-destructive.

Now we are letting the PIG play a big part in the game. The PIG will do whatever it takes to feed the Ego, right now, with no regard to annoying details like ability to pay later. The Egoic mind may even rationalize the borrowing by telling us that if we measure up to other people's material standards, they will then hold us in higher regard, and we'll get the job or promotion that enables us to not only pay off the debt but spend on other cool things, too. But what happens more often is that the monthly payments and interest add up until our finances are out of control — leading to stress, unhappiness, and strain on our relationships.

I included the anecdote about the temple because charitable giving can be another form of using money to feed the Ego, and there are differing opinions about it. Some people say motivations don't matter as long as the cause is good, while others say giving should only be done selflessly in the purest spirit, with no desire for recognition or any *quid pro quo.*

My view is that motivation does matter, but that striving to be pure and saintly can become an Ego goal in itself and may not always be realistic. To me, a healthy option is what I call "enlightened self-giving." This is giving done from full awareness — giving for the highest good of all, while knowing that in the process, something may come back to you, including recognition. If you're doing it for the *quid pro quo,* then it becomes a transaction, a deal more than a gift.

Awareness of our motivations is really the key to all aspects of managing money. It can prevent us from going into debt to feed our Egos. It can show us how to use money to begin building lasting happiness, and achieve "success" on terms that hold genuine value for ourselves and others.

.

Questions for Learning: Start to ask yourself why you want the things you are spending money on — is it because the big YOU wants them? Are they enriching your daily life and the lives of those around you? Or is what you're getting for your money nothing more than an ephemeral Ego boost?

LIFE SPACE: YOUR MONEY / Level 3

WARREN BUFFETT, THE PERSON

Although many people have heard of Warren Buffet the billionaire, the investor, and the CEO of Berkshire Hathaway, few are familiar with Warren Buffett the person — a role, I would argue, that is more inspirational than all of the others combined. The financial returns from the shares of stock that I own in his company are not nearly as valuable to me as what I've been able to learn about his life and his own attitudes towards money.

As I write this, Warren Buffett is 80 years old. A couple of years ago he was ranked as the wealthiest person in the world. He is currently number 3 on the list with a net worth of over $45 billion, an immense sum that places him far above many well-known people regarded as fabulously wealthy in their own right. But I would call your attention to some other qualities that make him stand out.

The first is simply how well and widely he is liked. Throughout history, extremely wealthy men have typically been individuals who evoked fiercely divided opinions. So it has been with John D. Rockefeller and many more, up to modern times. They are seen as heroes by some, but also by others as villains or as distasteful characters, either due to their business tactics, their attempts to use wealth for power, or just their personalities.

Not so with Warren Buffett. I can't think of another richest-of-the-rich type who is so *universally* admired, by people with all sorts of social and political views. And if we look closer we can begin to see why.

While some billionaires flaunt their wealth extravagantly, Buffett maintains the same down-to-earth lifestyle he has long been content with. Born in Omaha, Nebraska, he still lives in the same five-bedroom house he bought in 1957 for $31,500. He still drives himself to and from work, still stops to eat at the local Dairy Queen … and at the same time, despite these modest habits, he isn't known as a pathologically penny-pinching Scrooge, either. By all accounts he neither feels a need to show off his wealth nor to hoard it jealously.

This clear-headedness and healthy balance have also been evident in his investing and business practices. Some people try to get rich by becoming hard-driving, ruthless predators, while others think the key is to spot hot trends in the market and jump in quick, scoring a big hit. Here again, Warren Buffett does neither. He invests in companies on the basis of sound business fundamentals — not because he thinks he can squeeze money out of them by chopping them into pieces or running them dry, or because they're in hot new industries, but because they are well-run firms that can continue being good businesses. And wouldn't you know, by being a guy who doesn't go for the quick bucks, he has made bigger bucks than anyone while enabling many others to earn a living, too.

Finally, I and others admire Warren Buffett's approach to charitable giving. Except for a certain amount that goes to his heirs, he has pledged to give away virtually all of his fortune. In one interview he said he "agreed with Andrew Carnegie, who said that huge fortunes that flow in large part from society should in large part be returned to society."

And what's striking is how Buffett chose to give. The common practice among the very wealthy is to give in ways that perpetuate their names and their legacies. They establish grant-making foundations that carry their names. They build universities and hospitals named for themselves, or set up funds to award high-profile scholarships in their names. Much good is done through such giving, of course — and it also assures that we won't soon forget the donor behind the good work.

Warren Buffett did something utterly different. In 2006, he announced that the bulk of his fortune would be transferred into somebody else's foundation: the Bill and Melinda Gates Foundation, to make that huge pool of charitable money even larger and to be given away under their names rather than his own! In the history of big-time philanthropy, this was unheard of.

A Healthy Relationship with Money

Buffett knows Bill and Melinda Gates personally, so he trusts them. More important, he saw practical benefits in creating a single extra-large foundation rather than having a separate one. The money could then be used more efficiently, and with greater strategic impact for doing good.

But it takes a truly "big" person to choose to go for those benefits, while passing up the glory that could come from building a charitable empire of one's own. I would say it takes the big YOU.

In all of Warren Buffett's dealings, what stands out most is that he does not seem to *identify* himself with his money. He is certainly interested in money — by all accounts, he's been fascinated by business and finance since childhood — but he also shows that he cares more about what he can do with money rather than what it can do for him.

When we try to use money to prove our worth or define our very existence, we are merely feeding our mind-made identities, our Egos. We are living as something that isn't us. In doing so, we may indeed "make our mark" in the world; the question is what kind of mark we want it to be. The healthiest marks and the happiest lives come from knowing what we really are, and using our money accordingly.

Question for Learning: Although you probably aren't as rich as Warren Buffett, what can you see in his ways of being and doing that you might apply to enrich your life — both financially, and as a person?

KIDS FOR SIGHT

Here is a story in which someone with very little money, limited abilities and experience was able to accomplish his childhood dream while still a child.

When my son Nyan — whose name means "vision" in Sanskrit — was just four years old, we were flipping through ORBIS International's annual report. ORBIS is a charity that we supported in his name, whose mission is to deliver sight-saving eye care worldwide. Nyan stopped me when he noticed a picture of Ronald McDonald, the clown. He asked me what the picture was about and I told him that Ronald was inaugurating a pediatric eye hospital for children in India.

Without blinking an eye, Nyan immediately proclaimed that he wanted to build an eye hospital too. Something in his voice seemed so serious that I asked him to repeat what he'd said. He told me, "Papa, I want to build an eye hospital in Hyderabad," the city his mother hails from.

Although my children were both born in the U.S., my wife and I grew up in India, a country with a large incidence of preventable blindness, a country where because of poverty and lack of medical training, every four minutes a child goes blind. It is believed that one-fifth of the world's blind people live in India.

Always a deeply compassionate child, Nyan found it unbearable to imagine that other children were not able to see their families and friends. This made him passionate to help. In 2006, for his eighth birthday, Nyan asked his friends to donate to ORBIS rather than bring gifts to his party. He collected $145. But Nyan knew he could do more, and with his younger sister Lehka aligning her mission of helping children to read with his mission of helping them to see, the two teamed up to make a difference.

We were invited by ORBIS to New York and learned about their plan to build 50 pediatric eye care centers in India by 2012. On World Sight Day, October 11, 2007, Nyan and Lehka officially launched their "Kids for Sight" campaign. With the support of teachers and friends, they set out to educate children about taking care of their eyes and invited them to join in helping save the sight of other children.

For their next two birthdays, Nyan and Lehka passed up getting gifts and contributed more than $1200 to their ORBIS project. Inspired by their vision and commitment, a large number of people all over the world including family, friends, community members, and charitable people began visiting their website www.kidsforsight.com. Donations small and large came in to support the cause. Although Nyan and Lehka did not reach their financial goal of $260,000, Kids for Sight raised over $53,000 to help build and open an ORBIS pediatric eye care center in Chennai, India — my home region, chosen because mom's home town of Hyderabad already had one.

The Chennai center was inaugurated in December of 2009. We had the awesome experience of touring the facility during a family trip home to India in the summer of 2010. In a mere eight months, the center had trained doctors and staff to detect eye infections early and had screened 36,000 children, treating 1,286. That was already more than a thousand kids who had a much better chance of keeping their sight in the years ahead.

The Best Answer

You would think I would be most proud of Nyan for this accomplishment, but the proudest I've ever been of him was during an interview with an ORBIS public-relations person, when he was eight years old. The PR woman had been talking to Nyan and Lehka about the Kids for Sight project. As her final question she asked, "So, do you want all of your friends to give to ORBIS?"

To the surprise of the interviewer and everyone else listening, Nyan thoughtfully responded with a "No." Then he added, "People can give to whomever they want. Because no matter who they give to, they'll only make the world a better place."

This told me that Nyan was acting from beyond his Ego. His subsequent actions, as well as those of his sister, confirmed to me that the two of them had motivations that were both stronger and more selfless than what most of us adults are typically driven by.

Children really, really look forward to receiving birthday gifts. Just giving up those gifts was noteworthy, and it wasn't easy for either Nyan or Lehka to follow through on their decisions. It helped that the decisions were truly theirs. We hear stories now of parents prodding their children or teens into starting charitable ventures, and even masterminding the whole thing for them, so the kids can have something eye-catching to put on their resumes for applying to college. This idea was Nyan's from the get-go. Lekha was inspired to join him. They got adult support for the steps they couldn't have done on their own, like launching a website and making arrangements with ORBIS, but they learned quickly as they went along.

Most important, this was truly a case of the kids having the *vision* to lead the adults, not being led by them and not being led by their own PIG desires or their Egos.

Question for Learning: Naturally children are "immature" in many respects when it comes to dealing with money. Yet there are times when people who don't have much money — including not only children, but a lot of adults — can be remarkably clear-sighted about how to use it most beneficially. At the end of the last story you were asked what you could learn from one of the world's richest people. What can you learn from those around you who have very little?

LIFE SPACE: YOUR CHILDREN / Level 1

A RUM-SOAKED CHERRY

Several years ago my business partner and I were in Silicon Valley working on a deal. After a very busy week, we decided to spend the Saturday before our flight back taking a side trip to Monterey Bay and Big Sur — beautiful areas along the coast, not far away. We arrived in Monterey ready for a nice, relaxed meal, and found a lovely little restaurant at the end of a pier. While we were enjoying the ocean view, sipping our drinks and watching the sea lions bask in the sun and fight over warm rocky spots, we kept getting distracted by the table adjacent to us.

At the table sat three men with a toddler who looked to be about four years old. The men had ordered the restaurant's famous "Flaming Bucket of Fire" — a large, colorful bucket containing a potent concoction of spirits, tropical fruit juices, and plump, red cherries. And as the men became increasingly jovial with each sip from their long, red straws, the toddler was becoming more and more insistent upon getting one of those cherries.

The boy began to scream and shriek. Too young to understand the concept of legal drinking age, all he knew was that adults were having something *he* wanted. It soon became clear that no amount of reasoning, cajoling, or pacifying would be able to calm the child down, and the dad wasn't making any move to take him away for a time out.

More and more patrons' eyes were fixed on the table as the commotion grew. Finally the father gave in to his child's demands, awarding him a bright and juicy, rum-soaked cherry.

Child's PIG + Dad's APE = Trouble

While we all have witnessed or experienced a child's tantrum, it's sad to see one end like this. The story illustrates the harmful effects that can occur during interactions between one person's PIG and another's APE.

The child's PIG — so intent on getting one of those cherries — could see nothing else but that goal, not the kid-friendly soda in front of him, not the placemat with crayons, and definitely not the fact that dad and his friends might have a point when they said the cherries were "not good for young kids."

Meanwhile, the father's APE was focused on avoiding discomfort — which in this case meant avoiding anything that would disrupt having a fun time out with the guys. When the child acted up, removing him from the restaurant until he calmed down was the obvious thing to do, but apparently dad's APE didn't let that idea get a foothold. After all, it would take dad away from the party. It would also mean facing a difficult one-on-one scene with an emotional little boy, and the APE doesn't like emotional difficulty: *That sounds like a painful experience!,* says the APE. Worse yet, the very act of leaving the table, with the boy in tow, might look and feel like publicly admitting defeat — as if dad was conceding that he had lost the front-line battle, and that he had to retreat to regroup.

That would be a blow to dad's manly Ego. More than anything, the APE wants to protect the Ego. Which is probably why dad finally gave in when all eyes in the restaurant began turning towards the table with looks of annoyance. On top of the disturbance to dad's little party, there was the added Ego-threat of public embarrassment. At that point, not only was the child screaming, but the father's APE was screaming: *Everybody's watching! They want you to make the kid shut up! Just do the easy thing, and give the boy's PIG a cherry!*

Although the father's decision did pacify the toddler for the short period of time they were in the restaurant, think of the consequences that such actions set up for the future. The father began by drawing a strict line about the use of alcohol by his child, then he allowed that line to be crossed. This alone could set an unhealthy precedent. And more troubling overall is the conditioning that's produced by giving in to tantrums. The child is learning to follow his PIG and learning that it "works." He's learning to throw a fit to get what he wants. At the same time, the father is conditioning himself to take the easy way out — the APE's pain-reducing and Ego-protecting way out — while avoiding the difficulties that come with truly caring for a child.

Questions for Learning: Even if you don't give in to tantrums, there are many other ways a parent can be pressured into letting a child do something unwise. What pushes your buttons? Are there times you choose the easy way out as a parent, despite knowing that it's not the healthiest choice for your child or yourself?

LIFE SPACE: YOUR CHILDREN / Level 2

'HE'S IN A BETTER PLACE'

My house in the suburbs of Pittsburgh is surrounded by a beautiful, sloping lawn. Our children take delight in the animals they can see out there: deer from the nearby woods, the occasional wild turkey strutting across the grass, and plenty of cute bunny rabbits hopping about.

Rabbits being small animals that are prey for others, such as the hawks in the sky, they are ever wary of danger. Unluckily, one rabbit's survival instinct worked against him. The rabbit was down a hole in our neighbor's lawn when the neighbor's son started the lawnmower. Hearing the dreadful noise approaching overhead — and probably feeling the rumble, too — the rabbit apparently decided it was time to run instead of hide. Up he came, right into the path of the mower.

Our own ten-year-old son cried out and ran to the scene. My wife, who told me about the incident later, heard the commotion and followed. Our son, the kind of boy who is always alert, wondered desperately if there was some way to repair the wounds and heal the fast-dying rabbit. But it was no use. He kneeled over the fallen creature, sobbing uncontrollably.

My wife, naturally, wanted to do something to ease the pain. She told our son, "Don't worry. He's in a better place."

And what our son did next was remarkable. He looked up, looked his mother square in the eyes and asked: "Are you telling me that the world is dangerous?"

I can only imagine the chain of reasoning that must have led him to ask this, but as parents my wife and I both know what a response of this type means. It means that instead of saying the magic words it's time to have a real conversation with the child.

What the Magic Words Really Say

Of course my wife felt compelled to say what she said. We've probably all said the same words or their equivalent at some time. When an animal dies, and much more so when a person dies, of course we want to comfort those who are grieving. Furthermore, many of us firmly believe that our souls will go to another, better place beyond this material world. Many of those we wish to comfort believe it as well. Yet it rarely helps to speak the magic words.

The magic words ring hollow because they come from voices within us that mainly want to ease our own discomfort. The Ego, especially a parent's Ego, needs to feel in control of the situation. The APE, the avoider of painful experiences, wants to smooth over the upset and have everything be all right, right now. But that cannot be done at a time like a death, when everything is not all right — for even if the departed has gone to a better place, those left behind still experience the loss, along with other unhappy thoughts and feelings.

Children can often notice this with greater clarity than adults. Perhaps as we "mature" our Egos get more firmly entrenched, our APEs grow more adept at avoidance, and our minds grow used to spinning the veils of thoughts and words that obscure what is. But there is no escaping the fact that we all die and we all suffer losses, sometimes quite unexpectedly. And in that sense, yes, the world may be considered "dangerous"!

Questions for Learning: If the hard facts cannot be smoothed over or avoided, then what is the healthy response to a child faced with the death of another? What would help the child develop a healthy attitude of his or her own? How would the big YOU respond?

LIFE SPACE: YOUR CHILDREN / Level 2

GOING FOR THE GRADES

As the parents of two school-age children, my wife and I have been on a mission to help them develop the qualities we believe they need, not only to do well in school but to flourish in life and contribute to the world they will live in. Chief among these qualities are a strong work ethic and a desire to learn. Sometimes, though, we find that our tactics are teaching the wrong lessons.

In trying to motivate our children, we've often said things like, "Finish your homework and then you can go outside and play," or "Finish your homework and then you can watch TV." Phrasing things in that manner only made our kids focus on the act of getting the assignment done, rather than on actually learning or understanding anything.

For quite some time we thought both kids were doing fine. They were getting their homework done quickly, but correctly. At the end of each grading period at school, they were receiving high grades in all of their courses. We came to realize something wasn't right, however, when they could not apply or connect what they supposedly had been "learning."

This lively girl and boy of ours would bring home A's in math, then falter when we invited them to use their math to solve simple problems related to everyday activities around the house. They would score A's in history or science, but when asked about the topics they had been studying, they'd have a hard time "connecting the dots" — explaining how the various factoids and ideas were related to one another, or to reality.

In short, their comprehension of the material did not match up with their grades.

We've also heard some friends say things to their children like, "You can keep your Wii as long as you get straight A's — one B and we take it away." The approach is a little different from ours, threatening punishment instead of offering rewards, but in my view these parents are making the same mistake we did: judging their kids' abilities by looking at the grades.

What are we teaching?

I believe that we as a society have gotten off track in this regard. We have no problem letting our kids immerse themselves in all sorts of digital fantasy games as long as their grades do not suffer. We are implicitly telling them it's OK to rush their work, cranking it out mechanically, as long as they get the grades. We establish grades and scores as the gold standard for learning — seldom questioning whether there is any direct correlation between grades and a child's ability to solve real-world problems.

I am sure you have had frustrating situations at work, or as a customer in stores and businesses, where the people on the job have no idea how to solve a problem. Many of these employees were once "good students" as determined by their grades.

The trouble lies in what we are teaching our kids to be motivated by. As we saw in Chapter 8 of this book, it has been found that "intrinsic motivation" is superior to "extrinsic motivation."

When people do their work for the rewards intrinsic to the work itself — the joy of engaging with it, the satisfaction of really getting to the heart of it — then they are on the path to becoming masters of that type of work. They're *into* it.

But when people do their work mainly for some other reward, then the work becomes just a means to an end. They're not really into it. Instead of learning how to work at a level of deep understanding, they'll be focused on learning how to "work the system" — how to satisfy the requirements for getting the prize, as quickly and easily as possible.

That's what my wife and I, and some of our friends, were conditioning our children to do. And it's a game in which everybody learns to let themselves be run by their inner creatures. Kids learn to get their homework out of the way fast because the PIG is squirming to go out and play. They learn to listen to the APE, who sees schoolwork as a difficult task to be avoided — unless the parents' nagging or the threat of losing a toy becomes even more painful, at which point the APE grumbles, *All right, all right, we'll do the work.* Then finally, if the result is a good grade, everybody's Ego is gratified. The kids are certified as good students, the parents as good parents and the teachers as teachers who got the results. Since these are very pleasing identities to have, seldom does anybody bother to wonder how firmly they are grounded in reality.

Of course there are students who do develop a firm foundation. When they get good grades, the grades come as a byproduct of actual learning. I fear, however, that too often the pattern is the one I've just described, and the pattern can be hard to break because our society is basically built upon reward metrics such as grades. Your SAT or ACT score has a lot to do with what college you'll get into. In business, the revenue from the last quarter has a lot to do with whether you will be receiving that bonus. And children catch on quickly. They learn that superficial work and corner-cutting are completely acceptable if they can just score the points to get the prize — never suspecting that they could be genuinely successful and have more deeply rewarding, profoundly happy lives by going about it another way.

Questions for Learning: What are the motivations for learning in your home? Have you been aware of them? Could a higher level of awareness lead to "higher education" for all concerned?

LIFE SPACE: YOUR CHILDREN / Level 3

LEAVING A FIELD
THAT WAS MY DREAM

When my son was two years old and someone would ask him where his father was, he would point to the phone. Although this seemed amusing to our friends, I was disturbed when my wife told me about it. The little guy wasn't too far off.

My work situation at the time was very demanding. I had started a high-tech company with a new product that had a lot of promise, then did what many such entrepreneurs do — sold the business to another company and took a position at that company, to grow the customer base for the product. While I no longer had the duties of being the owner, the job required long hours at the office and two or more days of travel each week. My office wasn't conveniently located, either. The company that had acquired mine was in Madison, Wisconsin, about 600 miles from our home in Pittsburgh. Although I talked to my family most nights I was away, it was clear this solution was not working out.

And yet, I did nothing about it. I continued to work the long hours and spend more time absent from home. I reasoned that I was doing it for the right reasons — selfless reasons, in fact, as the job allowed me to provide the best possible standard of living for my family. I rationalized that even if my son couldn't understand this now, surely he would realize the sacrifice I had made for him later on in life. Maybe he would even thank me.

But looking back, I probably kept that job more for the recognition it brought me. My product and company were in the streaming media industry, which was just emerging at the time, and I was regarded as one of the pioneers in the field. An important person like me couldn't walk away from the scene, could he? I don't know how much longer my delusions would have continued, and how much more our family dynamic would have deteriorated, had not my daughter given me a wakeup call that I just couldn't ignore.

When she got to be around a year and a half old she started to avoid me. We would talk on the phone, but whenever I returned home, rather than welcome me with open arms she would stand in a corner and not talk to me for at least an hour. As heart-wrenching as it had been to hear about my son's behavior over the phone issue, seeing my daughter act this way right in front of me left no doubt that I had to change my work situation soon or there would be serious consequences.

Following through with my decision was difficult at first. After leaving the Wisconsin company I could not find a suitable job in my specialty in Pittsburgh, so I took an executive position locally with a big firm in another field. My office was just a short drive from home ... but this job also required long hours and travel, and I still had very little time for my family! Would I have to change again? The difficulties, however, proved to be a blessing in disguise. They made me reevaluate what I really wanted to do with my life, and that is how I realized my true calling: to be a life coach.

Many of my good friends and well-wishers counseled me against it. "You went to IIT!" (the prestigious Indian Institute of

Technology), they said. "You should move to another city where there are more opportunities. You are wasting your life."

My choice to ignore them and stay in Pittsburgh was not based on career or financial opportunities, but on how my family felt about our city, our neighborhood and the sense of belonging that made us feel at home. Today I am lucky enough to be an executive and life coach at a progressive financial services company. And I have most evenings and weekends free to spend quality time with my children and wife.

The Real Deal

Over the course of my career change, I reflected on my motivations and came to realize that for a long time my PIG had been in control, busy feeding my Ego. In fact my initial decision to start a company — the step that had made my career take off in the first place — had been driven, in large part, by an odd snub that I had received several years before.

Back then I held a job that paid a modest salary. Charitable donations were needed for an education project that I cared about, so I decided to write a large check. To my surprise, the development officer wouldn't accept it. He gently explained that a person at my income level really couldn't afford to give that much.

This hurt my Ego and to satisfy it, I resolved to launch a start-up that would generate enough wealth to let me give to charity as I saw fit. While the motivation may sound high and noble, I now know that my PIG and Ego got entangled in the pursuit. The drive for fame and fortune became so powerful that by the time we had children, I even saw them through the lens of this inner craving. I justified my neglect by thinking of how well I was "caring" for their livelihood.

And although there were strong signs I needed to change my work-life balance, my APE let my dysfunctional lifestyle go on for far too long. Succumbing to the APE, I avoided the painful and scary experience of searching for a new job in a new industry and taking a big cut in compensation.

What made me change course at last was simply being aware of myself, my children, and how my choices were affecting them. My daughter made it so clear I couldn't miss it. While it's sad that I allowed things to reach that stage, I was fortunate to be able to respond by making some positive changes. And I was extremely fortunate to have a daughter, son, and wife who were at a level of being that enabled them to open their hearts instead of holding resentments.

Our home life today isn't perfect — nobody's is — and neither am I or my family members perfect. What we have is a home in which parents and children inspire one another daily to live from the lovingness of the big YOU. My wife and I still "run" the household in the sense of making the decisions that adults are most suited to make, but the big difference for me is knowing that I can function as a parent from a greater awareness — including awareness of how my personal choices affect my children, and awareness that I can learn from them every bit as much as they may learn from me.

Questions for Learning: Where do you stand, as a parent, in terms of awareness? Have you tried measuring how good a job you're doing as a parent not by the material things you can provide, or even by how much time you spend with a child — some parents must inevitably be away from their children for long periods — but simply by the nature of the awareness and love you bring to the relationship? Are you aware of anything you might want to change, on your end?

COMPLETING AND EXPANDING THE CIRCLE

MOVING MOUNTAINS

When I decided to go into life coaching as my calling, I consulted several experienced coaches to get their take on it. One such person, who was the most objective and clear, was Sharon Eakes. She is a professional psychologist and executive coach as well as the wife and business partner of Hal Williamson, the "happiest man" you read about earlier.

In January of 2011, Sharon sent me an email with a New Year greeting. What caught my eye, and moved me deeply, was the part describing what she and Hal had been up to over the holiday season:

This holiday was totally taken over for us by the birth of Fianna, the spectacular baby adopted by my son Gordon and his wife Kathleen. We were able to be there for the birth. It was an amazingly wonderful, complex situation, as you can guess, where love and good wishes for a child trumped every other thing in the world. I will be inspired by the experience for years to come. Here's what I wrote about it the morning we got home:

This may have been the most extraordinary experience of my life. It approaches mythic proportions, including a dream as big as life itself, an arduous journey of many parts, emotions as deep and wide as an ocean, uncertainties that threaten to choke off breathing. It is a story of many, many people helping things go

right. It includes systems within systems, working together flaw-
lessly: A loving couple eager to become parents, a calm young
pregnant woman and her attentive boyfriend, their two children,
the boyfriend's supportive mother, sisters and grandmothers, a
women's hospital awarded the best place to work in a large geo-
graphic area. It is a story of the birth of a baby, a spectacular baby
girl with lots of spun gold hair, Fianna, whom one nurse dubbed
The Christmas Angel.

The story includes a skilled and humane lawyer who drove
several hours in a neck brace to take the important legal steps
required in an adoption, and the bureaucracy of two states that
miraculously did in two days what can take two weeks so that
this new baby and her family could be home for Christmas. This
was the coming together of three extended families who found out
what happens when people treat each other gently, respectfully,
as people. The heart keeps expanding and the ripples go to the
ends of the earth. It may seem that I make too much of this, but
it feels like this is the story of the redemption of mankind. It is a
riveting love story. For love of a newborn baby, people got outside
themselves and demonstrated that love has the power to do the
impossible.

How the World Can Work

Sharon's story is simply the best news I have read in a long, long
time. We don't need to know any more details beyond the few that
Sharon has given. You can easily imagine how trying such a situation could be for the people concerned.

I would only add the following. Where Sharon wrote that "people got outside themselves," we would say in the terms of this book that they went beyond the confines of being run by their inner creatures. People like the lawyer and the public officials went beyond the fear of disturbing their own comfort. The people at the heart of the story — the adopting parents and most of all the natural parents — seem to have made their choices from beyond the sphere of needing to feed or protect their own Egos, or else they could not have enabled the story to unfold as gracefully and lovingly as it did.

In previous stories we have moved through a progression of Life Spaces that have to do with our relations to ourselves, our partners, our children and others in our lives. This story ties them all together. It shows how an entire circle of people, operating at high levels in each one of the Life Spaces, can collaborate to write a far-reaching love story.

Questions for Learning: Is there a difficult situation in your life? Where can YOU begin to write a new story?

THE STORY THAT
COUNTS MOST: YOURS

There have been twenty-one stories in this section, a nice number, but not nearly enough to begin conveying the great wealth of human experience in this world: the many mistakes made and lessons learned; the many joys that spring from people becoming aware of who they are, and acting creatively for the good of all.

What about your story?

If you have acquired insights into your life from reading this book — insights that are leading you to make positive changes, or that help you to understand more clearly what you've already done — then it would be extremely valuable to have you share your experience.

Others can learn from what you are learning. Your story could touch lives around the world, helping point the way to happiness for people you have never met. It can also help me, as well as everyone I work with and speak to.

Perhaps you have found a unique way of applying or interpreting the principles of the book, or of using them in situations that aren't familiar to most of us. Or perhaps your story is just so simple, yet so universal, that it deserves to be shared because many, many others could identify with it and be illuminated by it.

The process is straightforward:

> ➤ To share your story with me *and also* with many others directly, post it either in the Amazon reviews section for this book, or under the "Your Stories" tab at www.krishnapendyala.com. Or in both places!

> ➤ If you'd like to share it *only* with me for now — and not with others unless I first get your permission — then check "keep your story private" box on the web form. If you write by hand, mail your story to me c/o Big YOU Media, 2942 Skyline Drive, Allison Park PA 15101, USA.

As for writing the story ...

That's pretty straightforward too. There is no need to follow the format of the stories in this book, though you're welcome to if you want. The most basic format for a story of personal growth is one that always works and it goes as follows: "This was the situation. This is what I realized, and did. And this is how things are different now."

To put it even more briefly, the basic structure is "the way it was, what I found out, and how my life has changed."

Those are the key things that people will want to know, so just tell me about them. In this format, you can describe how you're using principles and insights from the book to deal with a particular circumstance, or achieve something ... or to change a persistent habit or pattern ... or just to live in a more aware, and more joyous, state of being.

You'll find that by putting your story into writing for others, you deepen your own understanding. That's always the special bonus prize — in giving, you gain. I look forward to hearing from you.

ACKNOWLEDGEMENTS

This book has emerged over a period of thirteen years, evolving as I moved through several life stages. In the late 1990s I set out to write a book about defining success on one's own terms. That initial theme changed, and deepened, as I explored further on my inward odyssey. A key turning point came when it dawned on me that I was being led by an inner impostor who was pretending to be me. This awareness brought me the clarity to see my life differently, and to respond to the world in a much healthier way. It also brought the themes and content of the book to the form in which they are presented here.

Such a journey is intensely personal but it cannot be undertaken alone. Here I want to acknowledge a number of people who have helped me along the way. There may be others I have missed, but nevertheless am extremely grateful to.

I start by thanking Mike Vargo, the writer who helped with capturing my ideas and translating them into print. Mike also enhanced the quality of the book through additional research and stories he provided.

Now come the people who have inspired or guided me through life. Some are family members or longtime friends; others are amazing people I have gotten to know through meeting them on flights and other places. I sincerely believe that there are no accidents in our intelligent universe. Everything happens for a reason — though we often don't know the reason at the time.

I owe who I am to my Papa: my grandfather Dr. M. Muniswamy, who was my idol of service and humility.

My grandmother, Mythili Muniswamy, taught me courage and raised me with motherly love for my first five years of life when my mother was ill.

My parents, P.S. Rao and Lalitha, gave me the gift of life and taught me the meaning of sacrifice.

My brother, Sreenath "Pendy" Pendyala, inspires me with a work ethic and dedication that are second to none.

Eternal thanks to my loving wife Sangeetha, whose patience and devotion cannot be expressed in words. Her untiring support has afforded me the opportunity to always pursue my calling and will never be forgotten.

Grateful love to my son Nyan, whose vision, compassion and insights are things I learn from every day.

Joyful love to my daughter Lehka, whose healing ability, love and clarity of thought suggest that children operate at a higher level of consciousness than adults.

Loving thanks also to my extended family, who never really understood what I was up to, but supported me through the times.

And thanks to the dear friends who have contributed special gifts of kindness, including:

My college friends at the Indian Institute of Technology — Ratty, Shiv, Nicky, Shashi, Billy, and Ashok, who were there with unconditional friendship when I was disabled, and even pushed my car whenever it broke down while taking me to the movies.

The non-judgmental Jasi, for his unwavering support in my personal quest for answers.

Klaus, Meyu, and my uncle Ramgopal, who helped me discover the joy of photography and gave me something to be passionate about in life.

Bobby Saldanha, for helping me realize a flair for writing with his wonderful sense of humor and attitude towards life.

Dr. James Thompson, my graduate school advisor at Indiana State University, who essentially became my adopted father in the United States. Jim artfully channeled my energy and has taught me more than he will ever know or acknowledge.

My cosmic brother Jon, for his unquestioning trust and for guiding me in how to lead and teach with his loving feedback and friendship.

My special friend Linda, who opened my eyes in 1988 to see that I might be the source of my own problems.

Dr. Wilson and Arnold Bloch, who helped me see many blind spots to keep me grounded.

Howard Wactlar, who taught me the meaning of perception and spoke the best words that I ever heard from an employer: "I would like to see you better employed."

Thomas Levine, my business mentor and friend, who helped me learn the healthy way to do business in this turbulent world.

James Dias, my intellectual sparring partner for over a decade and someone I bounce ideas off on a weekly basis.

Kanth Miriyala, for his constant encouragement and faith in my abilities.

Sharon Eakes, for the courageous love that often makes her the only one who can call me to account and straighten me out.

Christy, Mouli, Colleen, Samy, Renuka, Sunder, Ray, Atul, Prem, Suzy and Venkat for their support and friendship.

Simrit Brar, for cultivating my sense of design and helping me see its value in everyday things.

Dr. James Tucker, who nurtured my desire to write this book and held me accountable for years.

Marc Allen, my publishing mentor and a source of inspiration.

Ashok Trivedi, who not only provided me the space and support to practice and create this work but also to finally realize it in print.

The people who helped at various stages in the conception, creation, production and promotion of this book — Matthew, Berni, Rupa, Razi, Dave, Blair, Jodi, Jeanette, Joe, Heather, Susie, April and Joyce — thank you!

To BreAnn Decesere, Rebecca Selah, Justin Cooper and Derik Rhodes, who gave the core team the necessary boost to push the project over the goal line.

In addition, I would like to thank all my colleagues at the places where I have worked: Columbia State Community College in

Tennessee, the Carnegie Mellon University School of Computer Science, and the companies Visual Symphony, MediaSite, Sonic Foundry, iGate, and Waldron Wealth Management. Among other things, these people shared their life experiences with me to help me learn and become a better coach.

The writings of several great human beings — Mahatma Gandhi, Albert Einstein, Nelson Mandela, and the authors Scott Peck, Stephen Covey, Marc Allen, Napoleon Hill, Wayne Dyer and Eckhart Tolle — helped me to believe in myself and validate my sanity.

My special gratitude goes to John Waldron, whose trust, support and friendship enabled me to pursue my calling as a life coach and share this with you.

Finally, I am grateful for everyone in this world who practices awareness in his or her own way, thereby helping to raise the consciousness of humankind. May we all learn joyfully from each other every day.

— Krishna Pendyala

ABOUT THE AUTHOR

Krishna Pendyala is a lifelong learner. His work as a life coach and author is grounded in more than 30 years of intense study of the human condition. He has followed a program of rigorous self-reflection and observation of others, backed by formal learning and constant reading — and his work is further informed by professional experience in a wide range of disciplines.

Born and raised in India, Krishna moved to the United States in 1984 for graduate studies, then stayed on to build a distinguished career in technology and business. After beginning his career in teaching and research, he founded two multimedia companies and developed MediaSite Live, the industry leading product for online lectures and webcasting. Since then, he has held executive leadership positions at other firms.

In the 1990s, Krishna also began speaking and leading seminars on personal growth and effectiveness. Starting with corporate audiences, he has branched into working with people in all walks of life, and into coaching individuals as well as groups. Major themes he has developed and taught include the principle of unlearning conditioned patterns of the past, the use of *emotional* logic, and — as seen in this book — the central role of inner awareness.

Along with independent work in these areas, Krishna's current position merges his passions for business and life coaching: he is the Chief Operating Officer and Coach at Waldron Wealth Management. In 2008, *Investment Advisor* magazine referred to him as a futurist and the harbinger of a new career path. His varied interests and eclectic pursuits have led to his being quoted on topics ranging from ego awareness to biometrics. Meanwhile, he has begun his next outreach project to follow up on the publication of *Beyond the PIG and the APE*. The ultimate goal is creating an enlightened society where inner awareness empowers people to thrive in harmony.

Krishna Pendyala has a bachelor's degree in civil engineering from the Indian Institute of Technology, Madras, and a master's in educational foundations and media technology from Indiana State University. He has attended executive management programs at Carnegie Mellon University and Harvard, taken the Curriculum for Living from Landmark Education, and continues to hone his coaching skills through practice, professional courses and personal study.

He is a Charter Member of TiE, the world's largest entrepreneurial network; a National Member of the National Association for Self-Esteem; the organizer of Pittsburgh NOW, a learning community devoted to attaining peace through presence; and the founder of Discover YOU, a group focused on raising inner levels of awareness.

To learn more, please visit www.krishnapendyala.com.

AN APPEAL TO THE READER

It is my sincere hope that you will gain practical benefit from this book. Its success will be measured not by the number of copies sold, but by the numbers of lives positively impacted. I would be very grateful if you would take the time to share your experiences after reading the book, by contacting me through my website at www.krishnapendyala.com or my Facebook page.

By sharing your experience, you help to build a global community of people creating happier and healthier lives. We each are on the path of bringing joy into our own life, and extending that joy to those around us. I now appeal to you to extend your reach even further by reaching out to share. Together, we can strive to make this world work better for all.

Any comments you have will be appreciated. If you wish to send a complete personal story, as suggested under "The Story That Counts Most," please do so ... but your feedback is valuable even if it's in some other form than a story, even a few brief lines. I would like to know where you are on the path to joy and fulfillment, and any specifics on how insights from the book were useful.

I was inspired to write this book to empower men and women to achieve lasting fulfillment, without protracted struggles or huge crises. I shared my journey and other true stories with you, in hopes that this will enable you to learn and grow in a way that is less painful and more direct than the path I took.

We can all learn from each others' mistakes and we wouldn't learn anything if it wasn't for making mistakes. My wish is to raise our awareness by sharing life experiences that we can all identify with — so that we can all learn to catch ourselves when we're in peril of allowing misguided inner drives and delusions to rule our lives.

Namaste,

Krishna

Made in the USA
San Bernardino, CA
30 September 2015